MARTYN LEWIS

SEASONS OF OUR LIVES

SPRING

THE PATH TO DISCOVERY

SUMMER

TO LOVE OR LET GO

AUTUMN

THE CHANGING MOODS

WINTER

CHRISTMAS

THE PLEASURE AND THE PARTING

First published in Great Britain in 1999 by
Lennard Publishing
a division of Lennard Associates Limited
Mackerye End, Harpenden
Hertfordshire AL5 5DR

A CIP catalogue record for this book
is available from the British Library

ISBN 1 85291 142 5

Illustrations throughout are reproduced with the permission of
Pocknell Studio - the designers from whose collection they are taken.
We apologise to anyone whom we have been unable to trace before
going to print.

Editor: Michael Leitch
Design: Pocknell Studio
Cover design: Paul Cooper
Cover photograph: Siân Trenberth/Wales Tourist Board
Typesetting: Cyclops Productions
Printed and bound in Great Britain by
Butler & Tanner Ltd, London and Frome

CONTENTS

To Liz, my literary conscience, with love

EDITOR'S NOTE

A single date after a main contributor's name
refers to the year of writing or the date of first
publication. Where we have been unable to
establish this, we have given the contributor's full
dates wherever possible.

INTRODUCTION

As a broadcaster whose business is words, I have long admired other people's! Reading, for me, is a never-ending journey - an unfolding voyage of delight and often surprise. I am continually captivated by the way a complex idea can be encapsulated in a few well-chosen phrases that arouse interest, emotion or satisfaction; a marriage of words and ideas that stimulates the senses, transports you instantly to another time and place - often familiar, sometimes not; or, as you look at the benchmarks of your own life, leaves you with the reassurance that you are not alone - that others have trod that path before, and left upon it a careful scattering of fine words to match every conceivable moment and emotion.

People write often about their dreams - of what might have been. They conjure a little help from their imaginations, but they write best about that which they have experienced. And the centuries have bequeathed a rich fund of writings about the human condition, revealing how some aspects of life have changed, and, more often, how many have not.

Choosing from literature's legacy is an awesome task - made easier by the personal nature of my selection, and the encouragement and help of my wife, Liz. And that personal brief also gives me an opportunity to include poetry from people who have touched my life in different ways. My elder daughter, Sylvie, now taking her first steps towards a career as a singer and song-writer, has adapted the powerful words of one of her latest songs, 'Tourist', about the difficult search for love. My step-mother-in-law, Venetia Carse, has allowed me to include a delightful short poem she penned about childhood ambition. From the charity, Age Concern, comes a moving appeal from an elderly lady to the nurses looking after her. Called simply 'Look Closer - See Me', it was found in her hospital locker after her death, and deserves a much wider audience. As does 'Slow Dance', a moving message to all of us with busy lives, from the powerful perspective of a young girl with cancer who has just six months to live. This poem was sent anonymously to that great newscaster, Andrew Gardner, and I am grateful to his wife, Marg, for allowing me to reprint it here after it was read out at Andrew's memorial service. As I sat there I thought of his typically kind gesture when I joined ITN as a very junior reporter in 1970, and the great man took the time to stride right across the newsroom from the News At Ten desk to give me a personal welcome. I can repay that now by giving further impetus to his wish that as many people as possible should read 'Slow Dance'.

The poem 'Last Letter', from a daughter to her father after his death, touches movingly on many of those thoughts which are often left unspoken in life. It was written by Barbara O'Hanlon as part of an epic romantic novel co-authored with her sister, my long-standing friend Stephanie Berke. The novel, *To My Daughter in France*, is gradually wending its way to (long overdue) publication, and is, in my opinion, going to have enormous impact.

There is also much here from people you already know and admire - not all as writers, and perhaps not for these particular words: Kingsley Amis and Roald Dahl being introduced to the facts of life; Simone de Beauvoir's very first love; John Arlott falling in love with cricket; Graham Greene meeting a friend he hadn't seen for thirty years; Hilaire Beloc savouring the strange things we eat; Jonathan Swift's resolutions 'when I come to be old'; Queen Victoria's delight at her 'dearest Albert'; Judi Dench's path to becoming an actress; Winston Churchill choosing his career; Pete Townshend of The Who's lyrics for the pop song 'Pictures of Lily' ; Jackie Stewart's schooldays spent struggling with undiagnosed dyslexia; John Mortimer's early eyesight problems offering him 'the safe blur of childhood'; Seamus Heaney on a youthful fascination with railways; and Laurie Lee's memories of his mother.

Here too are many moments when the famous and the familiar coincide. Within these pages you will find Shakespeare, Bunyan, Lear, Rousseau and Burns; Marlowe's invitation to 'Come Live With Me and Be My Love', the early reply to that from Sir Walter Ralegh, and another, more fitting to modern times, from Cecil Day Lewis; E E Cummings's delightfully daring 'May I feel? said he'; and Christina Rossetti's intensely moving 'Remember me when I am gone away'.

No book touching on so many different sides of life would be complete without the definitive wisdom of Rudyard Kipling's 'If', presented to me by Liz at a crossroads in my life when I needed it most. Nor could I omit the sense of early adventure in A A Milne's 'Now We Are Six'. One Christmas, when reading that aloud to my then very small daughters, I had just got to the part where Pooh says 'It isn't much fun for one, but two can stick together ...' when Sylvie interrupted. 'Daddy,' she asked in a VERY loud voice, 'can THREE stick together?' The laughter from the assembled throng encouraged further demonstrations of her newly learned ability to count. 'Can FOUR stick together? Can FIVE stick together?' And so on, until unacceptable levels of stickability were reached, and all attempts to finish the poem were abandoned!

So, for me, this book is an irresistible opportunity to pull together a file of diverse and delightful writings which often trigger personal memories, and will, hopefully, capture a mood or a moment for you too.

And through it all, in chasing the seasons of our lives, I have been at pains not to neglect the seasons of each year, which provide the physical backdrop for so much of our growing up and growing old. So here, too, the finest writers can transport you to balmy, lakeland summer days or to the streets of Swansea for 'A Child's Christmas in Wales'. And do forgive me for including a special chapter on Christmas. It is simply because most of my Christmases past have found me in carol concerts, reading from the rich tapestry of words that have been woven around this great celebration. So I felt this was a good opportunity to bring together what I consider to be the finest thoughts about Christmas, as seen by John Betjeman, Richmal Crompton, Charles Dickens, Kenneth Grahame and Dylan Thomas, amongst others.

There is, I believe, something for all of us in this book - and something *of* all of us too.

MARTYN LEWIS
September 1999

SPRINGTI

THE PATH

ME
TO DISCOVERY

FIRST MEMORIES

My first memory is of the brightness of light - light all around. I was sitting among pillows on a quilt on the ground - very large white pillows. The quilt was a cotton patchwork of two different kinds of material - white with very small red stars spotted over it quite close together, and black with a red and white flower on it. I was probably eight or nine months old. The quilt is partially a later memory, but I know it is the quilt I sat on that day.

This was all new to me - the brightness of light and pillows and a quilt and ground out beyond. My Mother sat on a bench

beside a long table, her back turned to me. A friend called Aunt
Winnie stood at the end of the table in profile. I don't
remember what my Mother looked like - probably because she
was familiar to me. Aunt Winnie had goldish hair done high on
top of her head - a big twist of blond hair and lots of curly bangs.
My Mother was dark with straight hair and I had never seen a
blond person. Aunt Winnie's dress was thin white material, a
little blue flower and a sprig of green patterned over it. The
bodice was close-fitting with long tight sleeves, the skirt straight
and plain in front and very full and puffed and ruffled at the
back - a long dress touching the ground all around, even trailing
a little extra long at the back.

    Years later I told my Mother that I could remember
something that I saw before I could walk. She laughed and said it
was impossible. So I described that scene - even to the details of
the material of Aunt Winnie's dress. She was much surprised and
finally - a bit unwillingly - acknowledged that I must be right,
particularly because she, too, remembered Winnie's dress.

GEORGIA O'KEEFFE 1976

Gradually I came to know where I was, and I tried to express my wants to those who could gratify them, yet could not, because my wants were inside me, and they were outside, nor had they any power of getting into my soul. And so I made movements and sounds, signs like my wants, the few I could, the best I could; for they were not really like my meaning. And when I was not obeyed, because people did not understand me, or because they would not do me harm, I was angry, because elders did not submit to me, because freemen would not slave for me, and I avenged myself on them by tears.
ST AUGUSTINE 354-430

I was born in the middle of a snowstorm on Saturday, 30 January 1937. My mother was in a maternity clinic in Blackheath, London, at the time, about six o'clock in the evening, and my father was fighting a duel with Laurence Olivier at the Old Vic. Laertes versus Hamlet. Someone signalled to my father from the wings 'It's a girl', and at the curtain call Olivier stepped forward and announced to the audience that Laertes had a daughter. My father was quietly rather proud of this story. He told it to my mother, and according to her Olivier said, 'Ladies and gentlemen, tonight a great actress has been born, Laertes has a daughter.'

The earliest memory I can recall in sharp focus, with sound and smell, is of an early summer morning in August 1940 when I was three years old. I am alone in a garden, eating a bowl of milk and Kellogg's Rice Krispies. The sun shines, the air smells cool, sweet and damp with the moisture from the grass and the leaves of a large chestnut tree. A few midges and flies hover; their buzzing and the popping noise from the Krispies are the only sounds breaking the silence. Suddenly a vast wailing fills the whole sky. A wooden sash-window on the top floor bangs up. Dulcie Shave, my baby brother's nurse, thrusts her head out and shouts 'Vanessa! Come indoors. Come indoors AT ONCE!'

The wailing came from a siren sounding the first air-raid warning I ever heard. My mother, Rachel, remembers us spending that afternoon, and every night for a week, in the basement while the bombs fell on the City and the densely populated East End of London. Rachel laid out mattresses on the floor, told stories by candle-light and sang baby Corin and me to sleep:

> Golden slumbers kiss your eyes,
> Smiles awake you when you rise.
> Sleep pretty darlings, do not cry,
> And I will sing a lull-a-by.

VANESSA REDGRAVE 1991

I would like to say that I was born on the Orient Express as my mother took her bi-monthly trip to Istanbul. Or that I was smuggled out of China as a tiny baby, wrapped in silk and hidden in the guard's van in a truck of geological specimens. However, I was born in Kensington in 1953, and moved shortly afterwards to Wimbledon, in the days when that was in the county of Surrey and London was a faraway place. My mother had a passion for moving, but she confined it to moving house and changing husbands. So between Kensington and Wimbledon there were actually four more homes which are of little relevance to my tale.

In Wimbledon, where a rusty tricycle and long walks were all that came to vary the humdrum routine of home and watching the girls with pink leotards under grey tunics tiptoe into the ballet school across the road, we shared a fence with the Newby family. Eric Newby was a man who was said to have 'travelled'. In those days, prior to my fourth birthday, I felt that I, too, had travelled, on account of my occasional forays on the 155 bus to such high-spots as Elys, the department store, and the Holy Cross

Convent, where my sisters, who were half-sisters, were at school.

On the Eastern front of our garden, a small crack in a wood knot provided a spy-hole on to the lawns and borders of our other neighbours, and these contrasted so astonishingly with our own ill-kept japonicas and sprawling fruit trees that I used to spend hours staring through this peep-hole into the glamorous world of afternoon teas and island bedding 'over there', in the first foreign country I was to long for. One day, aged three, I suppose, I was less disturbed than the kneeling gardener on the other side of the fence to find myself eyeball to eyeball with someone else. That was the first of many meetings with strangers who became close friends without the benefit - or handicap - of a formal introduction. This particular gentleman, for such he turned out to be, was called Simon, and he introduced the exotic element of snacks on golden plates to my weary, harried mother, and so won the hearts of her four unruly daughters. We were an all-female household, and our china was chipped from many family rows. LISA ST AUBIN DE TERAN 1989

My earliest memories are, first, of making my way through the paddock, among the long grass of June, with the sorrel and moon-daisies taller than my own head. I was perhaps three. The moon-daisies, if you gripped four or five stalks, would actually support your weight as you leaned backwards. Secondly, I remember lying in bed in the morning - my mother already up and gone - listening to a bird singing in the dew-glittering silver birch on the edge of the lawn. The bird sang, 'Bringing it! Bringing it! Bringing it! Marguerite! Marguerite! Knee-deep! Knee-deep! Wait! Wait! Wait! Wait!' It was, of course, a song-thrush, but I didn't know that then. I just felt it was beautiful - so vigorous and clear - and nothing to interrupt or stop it. RICHARD ADAMS 1990

THEIR MOTHER, THEIR FIRST LOVE

I was still young enough then to be sleeping with my Mother, which to me seemed life's whole purpose. We slept together in the first-floor bedroom on a flock-filled mattress in a bed of brass rods and curtains. Alone, at that time, of all the family, I was her chosen dream companion, chosen from all for her extra love; my right, so it seemed to me.

So in the ample night and the thickness of her hair, I consumed my fattened sleep, drowsed and nuzzling to her warmth of flesh, blessed by her bed and safety. From the width of the house and the separation of the day, we two then lay joined alone. That darkness to me was like the fruit of sloes, heavy and ripe to the touch ....

The sharing of her bed at that three-year-old time I expected to last for ever. I had never known, or could not recall, any night spent away from her. But I was growing fast; I was no longer the baby; brother Tony lay in wait in his cot. When I heard the first whispers of moving me to the boys' room, I simply couldn't believe it. Surely my Mother would never agree? How could she face night without me?

My sisters began by soothing and flattering; they said, 'You're a grown big man.' 'You'll be sleeping with Harold and Jack,' they said. 'Now what d'you think of that?' What was I supposed to think? - to me it seemed outrageous. I affected a brainstorm and won a few extra nights, my last nights in that downy bed. Then the girls changed their tune: 'It'll only be for a bit. You can come back to Mum later on.' I didn't quite believe them, but Mother was silent, so I gave up the struggle and went.

I was never recalled to my Mother's bed again. It was my first betrayal, my first dose of ageing hardness, my first lesson in the gentle, merciless rejection of women. Nothing more was said, and I accepted it. I grew a little tougher, a little colder, and

turned my attention more towards the outside world, which by now was emerging visibly through the mist .... LAURIE LEE 1959

My mother, Madame Henriette Gagnon, was a charming woman, and I was in love with her. I hasten to add that I lost her when I was seven years old. In loving her at the age of, perhaps, six (1789), I had exactly the same character as when, in 1828, I loved Alberthe de Rubempré with a mad passion. My way of starting on the quest for happiness had not changed at all in essentials, with this sole exception: that in what constitutes the physical side of love, I was what Caesar would be, if he came back to earth, with regard to the use of cannon and small arms. I should soon have learnt, and it would have changed nothing essential in my tactics.

I wanted to cover my mother with kisses, and for her to have no clothes on. She loved me passionately and often kissed me; I returned her kisses with such ardour that she was often obliged to go away. I abhorred my father when he came and interrupted our kisses. I always wanted to give them to her on her bosom. Be so good as to remember that I lost her, in childbed, when I was barely seven.

She was plump, and of an exquisite freshness; she was very pretty, and I think she was only rather short. She had an expression of perfect nobility and serenity; she was dark, vivacious, and surrounded by a regular court; she often forgot to give the orders to her three maidservants; and, to conclude, she used often to read in the original the *Divine Comedy* of Dante, of which I found long afterwards five or six different editions in her apartments, which had remained shut up since her death.

She perished in the flower of her youth and beauty; in 1790 she might have been twenty-eight or thirty years old. STENDHAL 1835-36

ADVENTURES

US TWO

Wherever I am, there's always Pooh,
There's always Pooh and Me.
Whatever I do, he wants to do,
'Where are you going to-day?' says Pooh:
Well, that's very odd 'cos I was too.
Let's go together,' says Pooh, says he,
'Let's go together,' says Pooh.

'What's twice eleven?' I said to Pooh.
('Twice what?' said Pooh to Me.)
'I *think* it ought to be twenty-two.'
'Just what I think myself,' said Pooh.
'It wasn't an easy sum to do,
But that's what it is,' said Pooh, said he.
'That's what it is,' said Pooh.

'Let's look for dragons,' I said to Pooh.
'Yes, let's,' said Pooh to Me.
We crossed the river and found a few -
'Yes, those are dragons all right,' said Pooh.
'As soon as I saw their beaks I knew.
That's what they are,' said Pooh, said he.
'That's what they are,' said Pooh.

'Let's frighten the dragons,' I said to Pooh.
'That's right,' said Pooh to Me.
'*I'm* not afraid,' I said to Pooh,
And I held his paw and I shouted 'Shoo!
Silly old dragons!' - and off they flew.
'I wasn't afraid,' said Pooh, said he,
'I'm *never* afraid with you.'

So wherever I am, there's always Pooh,
There's always Pooh and Me.
'What would I do?' I said to Pooh,
'If it wasn't for you,' and Pooh said: 'True,
It isn't much fun for One, but Two
Can stick together,' says Pooh, says he.
'That's how it is,' says Pooh.
A A MILNE 1926

I was nearly four, and the joy of running away became conscious. I set out with a mackintosh over my arm, my toothbrush and one penny halfpenny in its pocket, walking down the road to Plymouth to get into a ship and go to sea. The early stages, and whatever tale led up to this exploit are lost: but the white road is there with a film of dust upon it, swinging downhill, and the open, high, cathedral feeling of the world as the latch clicks the home-field gate behind me. And then a rather small feeling as I walk down the road alone. At the bottom of the hill, Mark the postman appears coming towards me, and asks what I do so far from home? 'Plymouth's a turrible long way,' he remarks. He thinks a penny halfpenny will not take me so far. He is very sympathetic. He suggests we might go home and collect a little more cash and start again. And I remember a rather warm pleasantness in the holding of his comfortable hand, and a tiresome amount of surprise shown by a group on the lawn. Running away is the wrong word for such adventures, that go not to escape but to seek. The beckoning counts, and not the clicking latch behind you: and all through life the actual moment of emancipation still holds that delight, of the whole world coming to meet you like a wave.
FREYA STARK 1950

THE RAILWAY CHILDREN

When we climbed the slopes of the cutting
We were eye-level with the white cups
Of the telegraph poles and the sizzling wires.

Like lovely freehand they curved for miles
East and miles west beyond us, sagging
Under their burden of swallows.

We were small and thought we knew nothing
Worth knowing. We thought words travelled the wires
In the shiny pouches of raindrops.

Each one seeded full with the light
Of the sky, the gleam of the lines, and ourselves
So infinitesimally scaled

We could stream through the eye of a needle.
SEAMUS HEANEY 1984

As children, we had strange pets .... At one time or another, we had monkeys, parakeets, falcons, frogs and toads, grass snakes, and a large African lizard who the cook killed with a poker in a moment of terror. My favourite was Gregorio, the sheep, who just missed crushing me when I was ten. I think we brought him from Italy when he was a baby. Poor Gregorio was always a misfit, a true 'black sheep'; the only thing he loved was Nene, the horse. Luis also had a hatbox filled with tiny grey mice whom he allowed us to look at once a day - well-fed, fairly comatose couples who procreated non-stop. Before he left for Madrid, he took them up to the attic and, much to our dismay, gave them their freedom while admonishing them to 'grow and multiply'.

We loved and respected all living creatures, even those from the vegetable kingdom, and I think they felt the same way about us. As children, we could walk through a forest crawling with wild animals and come out unscathed. There was one exception, however - spiders. These hideous and terrifying monsters threw us into an inexplicable panic; but given our Buñuelesque penchant for morbidity, they were often the main topic of conversation. And our stories about them are outrageous, like the one about Luis seeing an eight-eyed, jagged-toothed monster and fainting away at an inn in Toledo and coming to only after he was back in Madrid .... Spiders! Scorpions! Tarantulas! Our nightmares, like our dinner-table conversations, were filled with them. Conchita Buñuel 1982

THE TRIALS OF EARLY LIFE

It was Archie who again got the dirty end of the stick one day at a picnic in the botanical garden. Lunch over, he was settled down for his afternoon snooze while I went birds' nesting. The next thing that struck my startled eyes was Archie hoofing it across the lawns, followed by a rattlesnake in full cry and timpani. He tells me - and this I never realised - that he was woken from his slumber by the slimy creature oiling its way over his stomach. Alarmed, he was up and away, screaming with the thing at his heels. Minutes - perhaps only seconds - later the curtain came down on the drama as Pa beat the life out of the slithery intruder with a heavy stick.

A year or so later it was my turn to be unnerved. It was around tea-time, I think, that the two of us and some other kids staying in the hotel went out into the grounds playing at cowboys and Indians. In the process we ran across a little Indian boy in the undergrowth. All in fun and make-believe we captured him and tied him to a tree. I carried a toy rifle and, pretending to hit

the prisoner over the head with it, the wretched thing slipped in my hand and gave his skull a hearty crack. When blood began to course down his forehead and face the lot of us took to our heels in alarm leaving the unfortunate little victim still tied to the tree.

I recall dashing into the house to find Ma playing bridge with three other ladies. I stood silently beside her, not saying a word. Undoubtedly my insides were churning with anxiety at what I had done. Shortly one of the peons (servants) entered the room and asked to speak to my mother. What transpired between them later I never knew, but the peon, the father of the little Indian boy, had it in for me from then on. Obviously I had been marked down as the guilty party for what must have seemed like a savage assault.

The man served at meals and he never took his eyes off me as he went about his duties. He terrified the living daylights out of me with his hypnotic glare as I hung on to my guilty secret. A storm was building up inside him and I sensed it as I grew more and more frightened.

Then, one day, the storm broke as Arch and I were having our afternoon rest. Next to our bedroom there was a washroom where the ayah was busy with some laundry. Suddenly I was aware that the door handle was moving slowly and into the bedroom slowly crept the man, intent on revenge, with murder in his eyes and what appeared to be a chair leg in his hand. At my first scream of terror the ayah appeared from the bathroom, sized up the situation in a flash and leapt at the intruder. She fought him like a tigress protecting one of her cubs while I screamed the place down.

At that precise moment Ma and Pa happened to be passing the window as they set out for a walk. Hearing my shrieks, Papa hared back into the house and over-powered the man, who was dismissed forthwith. Whether he would have done me in I shall never know. Maybe he only intended a little blood-letting to square the account. The storm building up inside him for weeks may have got the upper hand and he might have finished the job but for the prompt action of that ayah.

Assuredly one lives on borrowed time. Double-pneumonia; a virulent epidemic of cholera escaped; a pernicious attack of dysentery lasting several months that could have been a killer; and, many years ahead, missing the Munich air crash - all these have provided a catalogue of escapes. GEOFFREY GREEN 1985

Eyesight was a problem for both of us. Up to the age of five I enjoyed the privileges of myopia, seeing the world in a glorious haze like an Impressionist painting. My contemporaries appeared blurred and attractive, grown-ups loomed in vague magnificence. I went daily to school and kept my eyes politely on the backboard where I could see only chalky confusion. After a year of this my mother noticed that my education was at a standstill and sent me to the oculist: the world sprang at me in hideous reality, full of people with open pores, blackheads and impetigo. A deep-focus moustache appeared on an art mistress whom I had considered beautiful. Flinching from this unusual clarity I went to school and sat in my usual place at the morning assembly, unrecognisable in a nose-pinching pair of wire-framed specs. The headmaster, whose awareness of his pupils was always somewhat vague, thought that this bespectacled intruder was a new boy. As I was too shy to disillusion him, I was put back in the bottom class to restart my unpromising academic career. I suppose I had become a new person, one who looked on life and actually saw it; but when faced with anything I am really reluctant to see, a pornographic film in the course of business, or an animal killed and plastered across the road, I still have the defence of taking off my glasses and returning the world to the safe blur of childhood. JOHN MORTIMER 1982

Few who saw them were likely to forget the arrival of the evacuee children. Some of the children, more from boredom than unhappiness, passed the time writing pathetic messages on the printed, franked postcards issued to them to notify their new address. 'Dear Mam, I want to come home. Pleas come and tack us home,' reads one surviving card, duly delivered next morning to a Liverpool mother. Only the postmark enlightened Mam as to her children's whereabouts. The writer had forgotten to include his address. 'Dear Mum, I hope you are well,' ran another card. 'I don't like the man's face. I don't like the lady's face much. Perhaps it will look better in daylight. I like the dog's face best .....'

I can vividly remember the crocodile of small children, laden with cases and gas masks, filing out of Newbury station and walking two by two up the road to the reception centre at the nearby council school. Some carried buckets and spades, for, to ease the pain of parting, their mothers had assured them that they were going to the seaside.

Many people still have bitter memories of the 'slave market', at which they were allocated to foster-parents - in one Lincolnshire town the cattle market was actually used as a distribution centre. A couple who took eighty children from Wembley to a village near Chard in Somerset noticed how the largest were immediately chosen by farmers needing unpaid help, the smallest being left to last. A thirteen-year-old Girl Guide in the village of High Broome, near Tunbridge Wells, noticed that smartly dressed little girls were soon 'spoken for', but 'a small tousled-haired boy, trousers too big, socks round his ankles, threadbare shirt and jacket and a small paper parcel of his belongings tied to his gas mask case', remained unclaimed for a long time.

The 'slave market' method at least avoided the sad trudge from door to door in search of a welcoming home. An Islington teacher was moved by the sight of a five-year-old girl who had kept cheerful all day, finally sinking down on the kerb of a Northamptonshire street in tears, and not even being consoled by the bar of chocolate in her bag. Before long, however, that 'lost feeling was cuddled away by the warm-hearted "aunt" '. Visiting her charges later that evening, the same teacher found them all happily tucked up in bed.

This was the general experience. The nation's mothers revealed on 1 September 1939, and the days immediately following it, a warmth and good nature towards other people's children that many of their guests still recall with affection nearly thirty years later. The inevitable childish accidents were accepted with exemplary patience. The daughter-in-law of a Yorkshire country vicar, then aged sixteen, recalls the arrival of two small girls, aged eleven and seven, from Sunderland.

They were very clean and well-behaved - 'especially selected for the Vicarage', she suspects - but the excitement, or the contrast between the vicarage food and their usual diet of pie and chips and bread and jam, proved too much for the younger one, who was immediately sick on the dining-room carpet. Both soon improved enormously in health and became much-loved members of the family, keeping in touch until they married.
NORMAN LONGMATE 1971

School began at nine o'clock, but the hamlet children set out on their mile-and-a-half walk there as soon as possible after their seven o'clock breakfast, partly because they liked plenty of time to play on the road and partly because their mothers wanted them out of the way before house-cleaning began.

Up the long, straight road they straggled, in twos and threes and in gangs, their flat, rush dinner-baskets over their shoulders and their shabby little coats on their arms against rain. In cold weather some of them carried two hot potatoes which had been in the oven, or in the ashes, all night, to warm their hands on the way and to serve as a light lunch on arrival.

They were strong, lusty children, let loose from control, and there was plenty of shouting, quarrelling, and often fighting among them. In more peaceful moments they would squat in the dust of the road and play marbles, or sit on a stone heap and play dibs with pebbles, or climb into the hedges after birds' nests or blackberries, or to pull long trails of bryony to wreathe round their hats. In winter they would slide on the ice on the puddles, or make snowballs - soft ones for their friends, and hard ones with a stone inside for their enemies.

After the first mile or so the dinner-baskets would be raided; or they would creep through the bars of the padlocked field gates for turnips to pare with the teeth and munch, or for handfuls of green pea shucks, or ears of wheat, to rub out the sweet, milky grain between the hands and devour. In spring they ate the young green from the hawthorn hedges, which they called 'bread and cheese', and sorrel leaves from the wayside, which they called 'sour grass', and in autumn there was an abundance of haws and blackberries and sloes and crab-apples for them to feast upon. There was always something to eat, and they ate, not so much because they were hungry as from habit and relish of the wild food ....

That Laura could already read when she went to school was never discovered. 'Do you know your ABC?' the mistress asked her on the first morning. 'Come, let me hear you say it: A - B - C -. '

'A - B - C - ' Laura began; but when she got to F she stumbled, for she had never memorised the letters in order. So she was placed in the class known as 'the babies' and joined in chanting the alphabet from A to Z. Alternatively they recited it backward, and Laura soon had that version by heart, for it rhymed:

Z-Y-X and W-V
U-T-S and R-Q-P

O-N-M and L-K-J
I-H-G and F-E-D
And C-B-A!

Once started, they were like a watch wound up, and went on
alone for hours. FLORA THOMPSON 1939

Because of my low standing in arithmetic, I was put at the
foot of my class. I remember this, and I have not
forgotten that while I sat there I felt a chill crawling up
my spine, like a beetle. Sickness, black and chill, attached the pit
of my stomach, and all the stamping feet and treble voices
coming closer were stabbing down into my ears, into my
throbbing head. It was the beginning of one of my nervous
headaches, and a cold sweat broke out while I struggled not to
disgrace myself by throwing up before my natural enemies,
strange children, on my first day at school. If the children had
been cannibals, and I a missionary prepared for the feast, my
doom could not have seemed more dreadful to me, or more
inevitable. Presently I should be sick on the bench: I should be
jeered out of school; I should be in eternal disgrace.

Then, suddenly, without the shadow of an approach,
destiny overtook me. A door opened; there was a thunder of
feet, a rumble of voices, a crowd of figures surged toward me,
hemming me in, shutting me out, with my headache, my
sickness. The older girls of the history class, like released colts,
brave, strong, fearless, with clear heads and quiet stomachs,
were thronging through to the schoolroom beyond.

Terror seized me, blind panic terror. A wave of darkness
rushed over me and I bit my lips till they hurt, in the frantic
effort not to disgrace myself. My ears rang; my elbows
quivered; my ice-cold hands even were afflicted by this agony
of physical shyness.

One of the older girls turned her head, as they tramped through the room, laughed maliciously, and whispered, 'Look at the white rabbit!' Mirth convulsed them. For the first time in my brief unhappy life I was an object of mirth, a figure for ridicule. Though I knew this was not wit, that it was not even sport, I felt the heart of a rabbit tremble and leap beneath the tucked pink and white cambric.

Flight remained. Flight could save me. Jumping down from the bench, I dashed out of the door, into the paved yard, through the gate, and down the empty street to my sure refuge with Mother. Mother alone knew. Mother alone understood. Mother alone could protect me from this despair of being different, of being outside the world. I heard calls. The class was on my track. Without turning my head, I could see with the inner eye the whole school pursuing ....

At the head of the steps my Mother waited with open arms to receive me. I flung myself upon her bosom, while the throbbing in my temples filled the world, filled the universe.

ELLEN GLASGOW 1955

At school you were labelled stupid, dumb and thick because you couldn't read or recite the alphabet. Even today, if you gave me £10 million, I couldn't run through the alphabet. I don't know the words of the Lord's Prayer and I don't know the words of my own National Anthem although I've stood while it has been played at many victory ceremonies. The wiring system is not right up there: it's not a man-made problem in the sense that I didn't concentrate or pay attention at school, it's just something that occurs to some extent in one in ten young people, and more in boys than girls. The humiliation, the mental abuse, the lack of self-esteem that you experience leave their mark forever, more so in those days because dyslexia wasn't properly recognised by the teachers.

I left school at 15 as a complete disaster, to the great relief of the school and much more to my own relief. It was a daily abuse, it was like somebody hitting you on the same spot everyday. When that happens the bruise gets bigger and the pain gets deeper.

There are so many young people still in that position today; they've got inferiority complexes, they're shy, they'll never look you in the eye, they'll avoid situations, they can't fill in a form. I couldn't fill in my driving-test form and I still can't fill in any forms, I need secretaries to do that sort of thing for me. But I'm lucky, God gave me hands, eyes and co-ordination that allowed me first of all to shoot, which gave me back some self-respect, and then to drive racing cars which brought new confidence. On the other hand I don't know anything about the history of my country; I know my geography because I've been to places, and I can look at a map of the world and identify where I've been, but I still don't have a great knowledge of the English language. The language that I understand today has been learned from conversation rather than from reading. JACKIE STEWART 1997

In the potting shed some weeks later, my friend, mindful of my education, disclosed the information that marriage was directly related to being bare, and that you couldn't get married unless you were prepared to be bare quite a lot of the time.

I was, of course, perfectly astonished by this intelligence, and somewhat disturbed. I was certain that nothing of the kind ever happened in our household, except when one occupied the bathroom, and even then the grown-ups locked the door.

My friend looked at me and I looked back at her.

'Bare?' I said. 'Why?'

She said that sometimes both of you had to be bare.

'You mean sitting having lunch, both bare?' I said. 'But supposing one of the dogs came in?'

She said: 'Dogs wouldn't notice, they're bare all the time. Anyway, it's mostly in the bedroom people do it.'

'Do what?' I said, and she whispered in my ear. My voice seemed absconded when it came out. I said: 'Are you sure? I mean what's the point of that? It sounds disgusting. I'm not going to let anyone do that to me, I can tell you.'

She shrugged, and I recklessly tore a scab off my knee which bled quite a lot, and I felt better. But it all sounded peculiar, and we didn't look at each other. My father's batman, Nunn, had taught me to snap my fingers, so I did some of that.

'Stop it!' she whispered. She was a bit older than me and had curly hair. Suddenly, I felt unsure that I really liked her, but I wanted to ask her something more. So I asked her what happened after people had finished doing it.

She said: 'They have cigarettes. Sometimes they have drinks as well.'

'Then what?' I said.

She looked at me and said: 'I think they sometimes do it again. So it must be quite nice. Probably.'

'Are they bare all this time?' I said.

She said: 'Well, of course, silly. They couldn't do it otherwise, could they?'

I didn't answer. Somehow, she made me feel uneasy, indeed most wretchedly discomposed. But, nonetheless, there was one more significant question I needed to ask.

'How do you know all this?' I asked.

'They left the door open once,' she said.

BENEDICTA LEIGH 1991

FALSE SECURITY

... I ran to the ironwork gateway of number seven
Secure at last on the lamplit fringe of Heaven.
Oh who can say how subtle and safe one feels

Shod in one's children's sandals from Daniel Neal's,
Clad in one's party clothes made of stuff from Heal's?
And who can still one's thrill at the candle shine
On cakes and ices and jelly and blackcurrant wine,
And the warm little feel of my hostess's hand in mine?
Can I forget my delight at the conjuring show?
And wasn't I proud that I was the last to go?
Too overexcited and pleased with myself to know
That the words I heard my hostess's mother employ
To a guest departing, would ever diminish my joy,
I WONDER WHERE JULIA FOUND THAT STRANGE,
RATHER COMMON LITTLE BOY?

JOHN BETJEMAN 1906-84

I must have been fourteen when the woman next door made in my hearing some very mild reference to somebody's honeymoon or some such depravity. My mother gave her a fierce (and absurdly visible) shake of the head. This state of affairs gravely impeded parts of social communication with chums' parents and the like. I must have been sixteen before my mother said, 'Well, I suppose by now you know all there is to know about marriage and so on,' and I said, 'Yes, I think so, Mum.' I liked her too much to add, 'but you'd have made my life a good bit easier if you'd said something like that to me about six years ago.'

As I have already implied, sex instruction in the home is often - usually? I don't know - not instruction but a formal permit. But it must be given. I shall never forget the scene when it came to my turn. I swear it began with me hearing my wife saying somewhere out of shot, 'Your father wants to speak to you in his study' - a room big enough, say, to accommodate a full-grown rhinoceros, though without giving him much room to turn round.

Philip and Martin came in, their expressions quite blank, innocent in every possible way that the most expensive film-director could have put there. They were, I suppose, seven and six years old. The short monologue I gave them slipped out of my head afterwards at the first opportunity, though I know I did conscientiously get in a certain amount of what might be called hard anatomy and concrete nouns, although again I must have used the word 'thing' a good deal and talked about Dad planting a seed. Well, what would you? I have never loved and admired them more than for the unruffled calm and seriousness with which they heard me out. I knew they knew, they knew I knew they knew and so on to the end but never mind. They left in a silence that they courteously prolonged until they were out of all hearing. It was a couple of years before Philip confided to me that he had muttered, 'Hold on to your hat - he's going to tell us the big one' as the two made their way to my 'study'. But we did it. In no sphere is it truer that it is necessary to say what it is unnecessary to say. KINGSLEY AMIS 1991

On one occasion during my first term, I went down to the matron's room to have some iodine put on a grazed knee and I didn't know you had to knock before you entered. I opened the door and walked right in, and there she was in the centre of the sick-room floor locked in some kind of an embrace with the Latin master, Mr Victor Corrado. They flew apart as I entered and both their faces went suddenly crimson.

'How dare you come in without knocking!' the matron shouted. 'Here I am trying to get something out of Mr Corrado's eye and in you burst and disturb the whole delicate operation!'

'I'm very sorry, Matron.'

'Go away and come back in five minutes!' she cried, and I shot out of the room like a bullet. ROALD DAHL 1984

I must here and now confess that I was completely and even scandalously uninterested in sex, until I was nearly grown-up. Shocking! Unnatural! you will say. Yes, certainly; I admit it; but then, think what a lot of trouble it saved. In fact, the only horrid curiosity I can remember, was a wish to know whether Keith at the dancing class had anything in the way of trousers under his kilt; and that was really only an interest in costume.

All inconvenient questions I used to put to Nana when I was in my bath. She must have been very clever at baffling them, for when I asked why one had toes, she answered at once: 'Well, you wouldn't like your foot to end in a sharp bone, would you?' ....

Another time I asked her what was the use of the interesting little button-hole in the middle of my tummy? 'That's where you were finished off,' she said. So I had a vision of God making a knot in the cotton before he broke it off to begin on another baby.

I don't know why this information made me think that babies (who apparently grew somehow inside) came out through this hole; but I did think so till I was nearly grown-up. And it still seems to me that it would be a much more sensible plan, than the complicated and painful exit arranged by the Management. But as time went on, I began to doubt the exactness of my deduction; and when I was seventeen or eighteen, I tried very hard, and quite unsuccessfully, to find out the truth about the matter from Chambers' Encyclopaedia. You can have no idea, if you have not tried, how difficult it is to find out anything whatever from an encyclopaedia, unless you know all about it already; and I did not even know what words to look up. Of course, I would have died sooner than have asked anyone about it; and I never did, but the truth just gradually dripped through, like coffee through a percolator ....

But though my sex-life was so sadly simple, there were things which shocked, nay, positively disgusted me. For instance,

I once saw, through the banisters at Down, one of my Darwin uncles give a friendly, conjugal kiss to my aunt, his wife. I rushed away in absolute horror from this unprecedented orgy. It seemed to me simply sickening, revolting, that this uncle - such a nice, quiet, decent sort of man - should be fond of his wife: fond enough of her to kiss her in the hall! Even now I can't bring myself to tell you which uncle it was. I tried never, never to think about it again. GWEN RAVERAT 1952

DEAR GOD

THE THOUGHTS OF CHILDREN

'Can you make church more fun? What about having a few videos? Just trying to help.' JENNIFER - AGED 9

'Why did you give Jesus such a hard time? My Dad is rough on me too, so I know what it's like. Maybe you both could go easy?' MARK - AGED 11

'I learned in school that you can make butterflies out of caterpillars. I think that's great. What can you do for my sister? She's ugly.' GREG - AGED 11

'When do you think it's OK to start going out with girls? How old were you when you went out with Mrs God? Did you kiss her on the first date?' WARREN - AGED 10

'I think you are super. Our priest says we are wrong if we think you are only in the clouds. He says you are here on Earth too. If it is OK with my mother, would you like to come to dinner on Tuesday night? We are having Lasagne. Hope you can make it.' MADELYN - AGED 9

'Do you have an extra plague for my sister like you did to the Egyptians? She's really stupid.' STANLEY - AGED 8

'A lot of people say there is too much rough and tough stuff on TV and too much killing too. I say there is too much rough and tough stuff and killing in the Bible.' DEREK - AGED 11

'I think you must be really clever to invent religion. That way you get all the people to look up to you and say your name a lot. I want to be famous too. My name is Frank.' FRANK - AGED 11

'Do you feel that scientists and politicians are to blame for nuclear weapons or are you willing to take on responsibility yourself?' JEROME - AGED 12

'Next time you send a flood could you send me a telegram beforehand? Mostly I've been good.' TED - AGED 12

YOUNG LOVE

In the Spring a young man's fancy lightly turns to thoughts of love. ALFRED LORD TENNYSON 1842

At fourteen Judith Johnson was quite simply the most beautiful creature I had ever seen. She had the face of an angel set on the body of a page-three girl and moved on legs that seemed to end somewhere near her armpits. I fell in love with her the first time I saw her.

Unfortunately for me this schoolboy crush was carried on from afar. I wasn't quite twelve at the time.

The relevance of this little piece of information is that for two glorious years until she left to work in the sausage factory across the road, her games periods coincided with my English lessons and provided that I could get into the classroom quick enough to grab a desk by the window, I could spend a whole hour just gazing at her, which I did.

I've never regretted those many hours spent watching her run around in her gymslip and tee shirt but during the months I've struggled to write this book I've often wished that I'd missed any other lesson than English. JOHN FRANCOME 1985

PICTURES OF LILY

I used to wake up in the mornings
I used to feel so bad
I got so sick of having sleepless nights
I went and told my Dad

He said, 'Son, now here's some little something
And stuck them on my wall
And now my nights ain't so lonely
In fact, I don't feel bad at all

Pictures of Lily
Made my life so wonderful
Pictures of Lily
Helped me sleep at night

Pictures of Lily solved my childhood problems
Pictures of Lily helped me feel all right
Pictures of Lily
Lily oh Lily
Lily oh Lily
Pictures of Lily

And then one day things weren't quite so fine
I fell in love with Lily
I asked my Dad where Lily I could find
He said, 'Son, now don't be silly.
She's been dead since 1929'
Oh how I cried that night
If only I'd been born in Lily's time
It would have been all right

Pictures of Lily
Made my life so wonderful
Pictures of Lily
Helped me sleep at night

Pictures of Lily solved my childhood problems
Pictures of Lily helped me feel all right
Pictures of Lily
Lily oh Lily
Lily oh Lily
Pictures of Lily

For me and Lily are together
In my dreams
And I ask you, 'Hey, mister,
Have you ever seen
Pictures of Lily?'
PETE TOWNSHEND 1967

Thursday April 8th
Maundy Thursday, Full Moon
Nose has gone down a bit.

My mother came home from her 'Well Woman' check in a
bad mood.

I allowed Pandora to visit me in my darkened bedroom.
We had a brilliant kissing session. Pandora was wearing her
mother's Janet Reger full-length silk slip under her dress and she
allowed me to touch the lace on the hem. I was more interested
in the lace near the shoulder straps but Pandora said, 'No
darling, we must wait until we've got our "O" levels.'

I pointed out to Pandora that all this sexual frustration is
playing havoc with my skin. But she said, 'If you really love me
you will wait.'

I said, 'If you really love me you wouldn't wait.'

She went then: she had to replace the Janet Reger slip
before her mother got back from work.

I have got thirty-eight spots: twenty-eight on my face and
rest on my shoulders. SUE TOWNSEND 1984

One day she (Mme Basile) went up to her room, bored with the stupid conversation of the clerk, leaving me in the back of the shop, where I did my work. When my small job was finished I followed her and, finding her door ajar, slipped in unperceived. She was beside the window at her embroidery, and facing that part of the room opposite the door. She could not see me come in nor, on account of the noise of carts in the street, could she hear me. She always dressed well, but that day her attire was almost coquettish. She was in a charming attitude, with her head slightly lowered to reveal the whiteness of her neck, and she had flowers in her beautifully brushed hair. Her whole form displayed a charm which I had ample time to dwell on and which deprived me of my senses. I threw myself on my knees just inside the door and held out my arms to her in an access of passion, quite certain that she could not hear me, and imagining that she could not see me. But over the chimney-piece was a mirror, which betrayed me. I do not know what effect this scene had upon her. She did not look at me or speak to me. But, half turning her head, she pointed with a simple movement of her finger to the mat at her feet. I trembled, cried out, and threw myself down where she had pointed, all in a single second. But what seems almost incredible is that I had not the courage to attempt anything more, or to say a single word. I dared not raise my eyes, nor even, despite my uncomfortable position, so much as touch her on the knee, to give myself a moment's support. I was motionless and dumb, but certainly not calm. Everything about me betrayed agitation, joy, gratitude, and ardent desire, uncertain of its object and restrained by a fear of displeasing, which my young heart could not dispel.

She seemed to me no calmer and no less timid than myself. Disturbed by my state, disconcerted at having provoked it, and beginning to realise the consequences of a gesture no doubt made without reflection, she neither drew me to her nor repulsed me. Indeed, she did not take her eyes from her work, and tried to behave as if she could not see me at her feet. But despite my stupidity I could not fail to realise that she shared my embarrassment and perhaps my desires, and was restrained by a bashfulness equal to my own. This, however, did not give me the strength to conquer my fears. Since she was five or six years older than myself, I thought that all the initiative ought to come from her and, as she did nothing to stimulate mine, I told myself that she had no wish for me to show any. Even today I think that I was right. For surely she had too much sense not to see that such a novice as I not only required encouragement but actual instruction. JEAN-JACQUES ROUSSEAU 1781-88

AMBITIONS - BUT WHAT TO DO?

'In order to succeed, we must first believe that we can.'
MICHAEL KORDA

'A ship in a harbour is safe, but that's not what ships are built for.' ANON

'Don't compromise yourself. You are all you've got.'
BETTY FORD

Use the talents you possess; for the woods would be very silent if no birds sang except the best.'
ANON

AMBITIONS

With coloured bricks
I shall build my Wall.
With firm foundations
wide and tall,
my Wall shall be
as tall as me;
or, p'rhaps,
no higher than my nose -
so's I can see the Grown-Ups pass
when I balance on my toes!
VENETIA CARSE 1997

I was now embarked on a military career. This orientation was entirely due to my collection of soldiers. I had ultimately nearly fifteen hundred. They were all of one size, all British, and organised as an infantry division with a cavalry brigade. My brother Jack commanded the hostile army. But by a Treaty for the Limitation of Armaments he was only allowed to have coloured troops; and they were not allowed to have artillery. Very important! I could muster myself only eighteen field guns - beside fortress pieces. But all the other services were complete - except one. It is what every army is always short of - transport. My father's old friend, Sir Henry Drummond Wolff, admiring my array, noticed this deficiency and provided a fund from which it was to some extent supplied.

The day came when my father himself paid a formal visit of inspection. All the troops were arranged in the correct formation of attack. He spent twenty minutes studying the scene - which was really impressive - with a keen eye and captivating smile. At the end he asked me if I would like to go into the Army. I thought it would be splendid to command an Army, so I said 'Yes' at once: and immediately I was taken at my word. For years I thought my father with his experience and flair had discerned in me the qualities of military genius. But I was told later that he had only come to the conclusion that I was not clever enough to go to the Bar. WINSTON S CHURCHILL 1930

39

I thought about this, and then I thought of all the things I wanted to do, the strange and beautiful places I've never seen, music I've never heard, books I've never read, new friends, new loves - and of how short life is. It was like a meal at the Shanghai - the awful anxiety of seeing so many delicious things cooling in front of one. Would there be the time, the appetite, the opportunity to taste them all?

I really don't know where to start but I know that I want everything and I want it now, with such an acute and all-consuming appetite that it gives me a dry mouth, a tingling tongue and a pain in the side of my head. JOAN WYNDHAM 1986

During that year, one enduring aspect of his entire life was deeply implanted. Opposite the school was the cricket ground - May's Bounty - named after Lieutenant-Colonel John May, the bibulous local brewer, who gave it to the town and the local grammar school. During the war, it had been used for various activities, important, no doubt, but quite unconnected with cricket. One summer afternoon, though, the boy came out of school and, hearing unfamiliar noises coming from 'the Folly', as the ground was called locally, he went, curiously, to see what was happening. There he saw men, some of them in white clothes, throwing balls at each other in netting cages and hitting them away. It was intriguing; he continued to go there, though there were not always men there. The appeal to omniscient Dad elicited the information that they were playing cricket. Then, one day there was no netting; the men were all in white, throwing and hitting; and suddenly one of them hit the ball up in the air, amazingly high, and another, running round under it, caught it. Then there was much more hitting and running and stopping and throwing. It was all puzzling, wonderful and, so far as his childish brain could assimilate, beautiful. He pestered Dad until an old (tennis) ball materialised; and Dad had shaped a piece of wood for a bat. Dad, though, was a swimmer, not a cricketer; he could bowl underarm, straight, but not like the men. It all helped, though; soon, too, he dared to sneak into the Folly and watch, silent and in some trepidation; but amazingly, no-one shooed him away - as most people did to boys in places where they had no business. Gradually the purpose of it all - or its basics - began to sink in. One day, too, Dad produced a hard red ball - they called it 'compo'. It hurt the boy's hands but Dad explained that was the way it had to be. The seed was sown. JOHN ARLOTT 1990

And how does a grown man feel about not fulfilling his role on earth but choosing to wait and hope and plead and cajole? How did it feel? Well, it felt as if I spent years in purgatory. A prison would have been heavenly by comparison, since then at least you have no choice. So I read and worked at my texts and trained and waited and went to classes and studied mime and took singing lessons from the kindly and most patient Mr Kuhn in Hanover Street, W1, and continued to fight with the dragon in my soul that was eating me alive. Then one day I said to myself that I would put a stop to all this once and for all. I would change the position I was in and be a guv'nor and be responsible for me. I would look for a play that I wished to do and call actors around me and ask them to join with me, at least to have a work-out and at most to put together our own work. So one day I did just that and for the first time I felt a rumbling deep down as I dug into the pit of my stomach for some courage to do it. STEVEN BERKOFF 1996

If you can keep your head when all about you
Are losing theirs and blaming it on you;
If you can trust yourself when all men doubt you,
But make allowance for their doubting too;
If you can wait and not be tired by waiting,
Or, being lied about, don't deal in lies,
Or, being hated, don't give way to hating,
And yet don't look too good, nor talk too wise;

If you can dream - and not make dreams your master;
If you can think - and not make thoughts your aim;
If you can meet with triumph and disaster
And treat those two imposters just the same;
If you can bear to hear the truth you've spoken
Twisted by knaves to make a trap for fools,
Or watch the things you gave your life to broken,
And stoop and build 'em up with worn-out tools;

If you can make one heap of all your winnings
And risk it on one turn of pitch-and-toss,
And lose, and start again at your beginnngs
And never breathe a word about your loss;
If you can force your heart and nerve and sinew
To serve your turn long after they are gone,
And so hold on when there is nothing in you
Except the Will which says to them: 'Hold on';

If you can talk with crowds and keep your virtue,
Or walk with kings - nor lose the common touch;
If neither foes nor loving friends can hurt you;
If all men count with you, but none too much;
If you can fill the unforgiving minute
With sixty seconds' worth of distance run -

Yours is the Earth and everything that's in it,
And - which is more - you'll be a Man my son!
RUDYARD KIPLING 1865-1936

WHO WOULD TRUE VALOUR SEE

Who would true valour see,
Let him come hither;
One here will constant be,
Come wind, come weather.
There's no discouragement
Shall make him once relent
His first avow'd intent.
To be a pilgrim.

Whoso beset him round
With dismal stories,
Do but themselves confound,
His strength the more is.
No lion can him fright,
He'll with a giant fight,
But he will have a right
To be a pilgrim.

Hobglobin, nor foul fiend,
Can daunt his spirit:
He knows he at the end
Shall life inherit.
Then fancies fly away,
He'll not fear what men say,
He'll labour night and day
To be a pilgrim.
JOHN BUNYAN 1695

SPRING - A TIME OF BIRTH AND REBIRTH

And like a skylit water stood
The bluebells in the azured wood.
A E HOUSMAN 1859-1936

THE SONG OF SOLOMON

My beloved spake, and said unto me, Rise up, my love, my fair
      one, and come away.
For lo, the winter is past, the rain is over, and gone.
The flowers appear on the earth, the time of the singing of birds is come,
      and the voice of the turtle is heard in our land.
The fig tree putteth forth her green figs, and the vines with the
      tender grape give a good smell.
Arise, my love, my fair one, and come away.
THE KING JAMES BIBLE 1611

THE TREES

The trees are coming into leaf
Like something almost being said;
The recent buds relax and spread,
Their greenness is a kind of grief.

Is it that they are born again
And we grow old? No, they die too.
Their yearly trick of looking new
Is written down in rings of grain.

Yet still the unresting castles thresh
In fullgrown thickness every May.
Last year is dead, they seem to say,
Begin afresh, afresh, afresh.
PHILIP LARKIN 1967

There is a sumptuous variety about the New England weather that compels the stranger's admiration - and regret. The weather is always doing something there; always attending strictly to business; always getting up new designs and trying them on the people to see how they will go. But it gets through more business in spring than in any other season. In the spring I have counted one hundred and thirty-six different kinds of weather inside of four-and-twenty hours. MARK TWAIN 1876

Loveliest of trees, the cherry now
Is hung with bloom along the bough,
And stands about the woodland ride
Wearing white for Eastertide.

Now, of my threescore years and ten,
Twenty will not come again,
And take from seventy springs a score,
It only leaves me fifty more.

And since to look at things in bloom
Fifty springs are little room,
About the woodlands I will go
To see the cherry hung with snow.
A E HOUSMAN 1887

SUMMER

TO LOVE

OR LET GO

LOVE'S BEGINNINGS

THE PASSIONATE SHEPHERD TO HIS LOVE

Come live with me and be my Love,

And we will all the pleasures prove

That hills and valleys, dales and fields,

Or woods or steepy mountain yields.

And we will sit upon the rocks,
And see the shepherds feed their flocks
By shallow rivers, to whose falls
Melodious birds sing madrigals.

And I will make thee beds of roses
And a thousand fragrant posies;
A cap of flowers, and a kirtle
Embroidered all with leaves of myrtle.

A gown made of the finest wool
Which from our pretty lambs we pull;
Fair-linèd slippers for the cold,
With buckles of the purest gold.

A belt of straw and ivy-buds
With coral clasps and amber studs:
And if these pleasures may thee move,
Come live with me and be my Love.

The shepherd swains shall dance and sing
For thy delight each May morning:
If these delights thy mind may move,
Then live with me and be my Love.

CHRISTOPHER MARLOWE 1564-93

HER REPLY

If all the world and love were young,
And truth in every shepherd's tongue,
These pretty pleasures might me move
To live with thee and be thy Love.

But Time drives flocks from field to fold;
When rivers rage and rocks grow cold;
And Philomel becometh dumb;
The rest complains of cares to come.

The flowers do fade, and wanton fields
To wayward Winter reckoning yields:
A honey tongue, a heart of gall,
Is fancy's spring, but sorrow's fall.

Thy gowns, thy shoes, thy beds of roses,
Thy cap, thy kirtle, and thy posies,
Soon break, soon wither - soon forgotten,
In folly ripe, in reason rotten.

Thy belt of straw and ivy-buds,
Thy coral clasps and amber studs,
All these in me no means can move
To come to thee and be thy Love.

But could youth last, and love still breed,
Had joys no date, nor age no need,
Then these delights my mind might move
To live with thee and be thy Love.

SIR WALTER RALEGH c1552-1618

Come, live with me and be my love,
And we will all the pleasures prove
Of peace and plenty, bed and board,
That chance employment may afford.

I'll handle dainties on the docks
And thou shalt read of summer frocks:
At evening by the sour canals
We'll hope to hear some madrigals.

Care on thy maiden brow shall put
A wreath of wrinkles, and thy foot
Be shod with pain: not silken dress
But toil shall tire thy loveliness.

Hunger shall make thy modest zone
And cheat fond death of all but bone -
If these delights thy mind may move,
Then live with me and be my love.
CECIL DAY LEWIS 1954

O, MY LUVE IS LIKE A RED, RED ROSE

O, my luve is like a red, red rose,
That's newly sprung in June:
O, my luve is like the melodie
That's sweetly played in tune.

As fair art thou, my bonnie lass,
So deep in luve am I;
And I will luve thee still, my dear,
Till a' the seas gang dry.

Till a' the seas gang dry, my dear,
And the rocks melt wi' the sun:
And I will luve thee still, my dear,
While the sands o' life shall run.

And fare thee weel, my only luve,
And fare thee weel a while!
And I will come again, my luve,
Tho' it were ten thousand mile!
ROBERT BURNS 1759-96

SONNET 18

Shall I compare thee to a summer's day?
Thou art more lovely and more temperate:
Rough winds do shake the darling buds of May,
And summer's lease hath all too short a date:
Sometime too hot the eye of heaven shies,
And often is his gold complexion dimmed;
And every fair from fair sometime declines,
By chance, or nature's changing course, untrimmed;
But thy eternal summer shall not fade,
Nor lose possession of that fair thou owest,
Nor shall death brag thou wander'st in his shade,
When in eternal lines to time thou growest;
So long as men can breathe, or eyes can see,
So long lives this, and this gives life to thee.
WILLIAM SHAKESPEARE 1609

STRAWBERRIES

There were never strawberries
like the ones we had
that sultry afternoon
sitting on the step
of the open french window
facing each other
your knees held in mine
the blue plates in our laps
the strawberries glistening
in the hot sunlight
we dipped them in sugar
looking at each other
not hurrying the feast
for one to come
the empty plates

laid on the stone together
with the two forks crossed
and I bent towards you
sweet in that air
in my arms
abandoned like a child
from your eager mouth
the taste of strawberries
in my memory
lean back again
let me love you
let the sun beat
on our forgetfulness
one hour of all
the heat intense
and summer lightning
on the Kilpatrick hills
let the storm wash the plates
EDWIN MORGAN 1920-

... But Glasgow days and grey weathers, when the rain
beat on the bus shelter and you leaned slightly
 against me, and the back of your hand touched
 my hand in the shadows, and nothing was said.
when your hair grazed mine accidentally as we
 talked in a café, yet not quite accidentally,
when I stole a glance at your face as we stood in a
 doorway and found I was afraid
of what might happen if I should never see it again,
when we met, and met, in spite of such differences
 in our lives,
and did the common things that in our feeling
became extraordinary, so that our first kiss

was like the winter morning moon, and as you
     shifted in my arms
it was the sea changing the shingle that changes it
as if for ever (but we are bound by nothing, but
     like smoke
to mist or light in water we move, and mix) -
O then it was a story as old as war or man,
and although we have not said it we know it,
and although we have not claimed it we do it,
and although we have not vowed it we keep it,
without a name to the end
EDWIN MORGAN 1968

FIRST LOVE
I ne'er was struck before that hour
With love so sudden and so sweet
Her face it bloomed like a sweet flower
And stole my heart away complete
My face turned pale a deadly pale
My legs refused to walk away
And when she looked what could I ail
My life and all seemed turned to clay

And then my blood rushed to my face
And took my eyesight quite away
The trees and bushes round the place
Seemed midnight at noon day
I could not see a single thing
Words from my eyes did start
They spoke as chords do from the string
And blood burnt round my heart

Are flowers the winter's choice
Is love's bed always snow
She seemed to hear my silent voice
Not love's appeals to know
I never saw so sweet a face
As that I stood before
My heart has left its dwelling place
And can return no more -
JOHN CLARE 1793-1864

I no longer asked myself what shall I do? There was everything to be done, everything I had formerly longed to do: to combat error, to find the truth, to tell it and expound it to the world, perhaps to help to change the world. I should need time and it would need hard work to keep to my purpose, if I meant keeping only a small part of the promises I had made myself: but that didn't frighten me. Nothing had been done: but everything was possible.

And then, I had been given a great chance: I suddenly didn't have to face this future all on my own. Until then, the men I had been fond of - Jacques, and to a lesser extent Herbaud - were of a different order from my own: they were detached, changeable, rather incoherent, stamped with a sort of fatal charm; it was impossible to communicate with them without reserves. Sartre corresponded exactly to the dream companion I had longed for since I was fifteen: he was the double in whom I found all my burning aspiration raised to the pitch of incandescence. I should always be able to share everything with him. When I left him at the beginning of August, I knew that he would never go out of my life again. SIMONE DE BEAUVOIR 1958

TO CELIA

Drink to me only with thine eyes,
And I will pledge with mine;
Or leave a kiss but in the cup
And I'll not look for wine.
The thirst that from the soul doth rise
Doth ask a drink divine;
But might I of Jove's nectar sup,
I would not change for thine.

I sent thee late a rosy wreath,
Not so much honouring thee
As giving it a hope that there
It could not withered be;
But thou thereon didst only breathe,
And sent'st it back to me;
Since when it grows, and smells, I swear,
Not of itself but thee!
BEN JONSON 1616

ELEGIE: TO HIS MISTRIS GOING TO BED

Come Madame, come, all rest my powers defie,
Until I labour, I in labour lie.
The foe oft-times having the foe in sight,
Is tir'd with standing though he never fight.
Off with that girdle, like heavens zone glistering,
But a far fairer world encompassing.
Unpin that spangled brest-plate, which you weare
That th'eyes of busy fooles may be stopt there:
Unlace your selfe, for that harmonious chime
Tells me from you that now 'tis your bed time.
Off with that happy huske, which I envye
That still can be, and still can stand so nigh.

Your gownes going off such beauteous state reveales
As when from flowery meades th'hills shadow steales.
Off with your wyrie coronet and showe
The hairy dyadem which on you doth growe.

Off with those shoes: and then safely tread
In this loves hallow'd temple, this soft bed.
In such white robes heavens Angels us'd to bee
Receiv'd by men; Thou Angel bring'st with thee
A heaven like Mahomets Paradise: and though
Ill spirits walk in white, we easily know,
By these Angels from an evill sprite:
They set our haires, but these the flesh upright.

Licence my roaving hands, and let them goe
Behind, before, above, between, below.
my America, my new founde lande,
My kingdome, safeliest when with one man man'd,
My myne of precious stones, My Emperee,
How blest am I in this discovering thee.
To enter in these bonds, is to be free,
Then where my hand is set my seal shall be.

Full nakedness, all joyes are due to thee.
As soules unbodied, bodies uncloth'd must bee
To taste whole joyes. Gems which you women use
Are as Atlanta's balls, cast in mens viewes,
That when a fooles eye lighteth on a gem
His earthly soule may covet theirs not them.

Like pictures, or like bookes gay coverings made
For laymen, are all women thus arraid;
Themselves are mystique books, which only wee
Whom their imputed grace will dignify

Must see reveal'd. Then since that I may knowe,
As liberally as to a midwife showe
Thy selfe: cast all, yea, this white linnen hence,
There is no pennance, much less innocence.
To teach thee, I am naked first: why then
What need'st thou have more covering than a man.

John Donne 1572-1631

A hot day. Stagnant, humid. By normal English standards really hot, insufferably hot. Not that England has standards about such things any more. Global warming no doubt. But it's a commonplace about growing old that there seem to be no standards any more. The Dog Days. With everything gone to the dogs.

Cheerless thought to be having on a pleasure jaunt, or what used to be one. For years now we've usually managed a treat for ourselves on really hot days, at home in the summer. We take the car along the bypass road from Oxford, for a mile or two, and twist abruptly off on to the verge - quite a tricky feat with fast moving traffic just behind. Sometimes there are hoots and shouts from passing cars who have had to brake at speed, but by that time we have jolted to a stop on the tussocky grass, locked the car, and crept through a gap in the hedge.

I remember the first time we did it, nearly forty-five years ago. We were on bicycles then, and there was little traffic on the unimproved road. Nor did we know where the river was exactly: we just thought it must be somewhere there. And with the ardour of comparative youth we wormed our way through the rank grass and sedge until we almost fell into it, or at least a branch of it. Crouching in the shelter of the reeds we tore our clothes off and slipped in like water-rats. A kingfisher flashed past our noses as we lay soundlessly in the dark sluggish current. A moment after we had crawled out and were drying ourselves on Iris's waist-slip a big pleasure boat chugged past within a few feet of the bank. The steersman, wearing a white cap, gazed intently ahead. Tobacco smoke mingled with the watery smell at the roots of the tall reeds.

I still have the waist-slip, I rediscovered it the other day, bunched up at the back of a drawer, stiff with powdery traces of dry mud. It is faded to a yellowish colour, with a wrinkled ribbon, once blue, decorating the hem. Could someone, later my wife, have indeed once worn such a garment? It looks like something preserved from the wardrobe of Marie Antoinette. I never gave it back to Iris after that occasion, and I think she forgot all about it. JOHN BAYLEY 1998

GAMES OF LOVE

She who is always in my thoughts prefers
Another man, and does not think of me.
Yet he seeks for another's love, not hers;
And some poor girl is grieving for my sake.
 Why then, the devil take
Both her and him; and love; and her; and me.
BHARTRHARI 7TH CENTURY

You smiled, you spoke, and I believed,
By every word and smile deceived.
Another man would hope no more;
Nor hope I what I hoped before:
But let not this last wish be vain;
Deceive, deceive me once again!
WALTER SAVAGE LANDOR 1775-1864

ELIZABETH IN ITALY

'Suddenly she slapped me, hard across the face.
I implored, but she declined to have any further
Social or sexual (so she put it) intercourse with me.
Neither would she give me either a personal picture
Or a lock of her most beautiful hair.
Indeed, she demanded, her exquisite voice
Quite hard, the return of her handkerchief
And any other things (I murmured, "mementoes",
But she repeated "things") I might have stolen
From her in my privileged position as her servant.
God only knew what had made her ask me
Fetch her the bathrobe that terrible night.
("That beautiful night," I recollected aloud.)
Did I believe our positions were reversed?
(I whitened at the accusation.) Well, then,
She wished to make clear now and for so long
As the relationship ("Madam!" cried I) lasted,
That it could only do so if I went to bed first,
Where she would come at her pleasure.
I could make no clearer sign of my heartfelt
Gratitude and infinite relief at these words
Than by the impassioned and repeated kissing,
There and then, of her magnificent left breast
Which had come out of hiding towards the end
Of her peroration. Whereupon she slapped me again.'
RICHARD WEBER 1932-

I, BEING BORN A WOMAN AND DISTRESSED

I, being born a woman and distressed
By all the needs and notions of my kind,
Am urged by your propinquity to find
Your person fair, and feel a certain zest

To bear your body's weight upon my breast:
So subtly is the fume of life designed,
To clarify the pulse and cloud the mind,
And leave me once again undone, possessed.
Think not for this, however, the poor treason
Of my stout blood against my staggering brain,
I shall remember you with love, or season
My scorn with pity, - let me make it plain:
I find this frenzy insufficient reason
For conversation when we meet again.
EDNA ST VINCENT MILLAY 1923

MAY I FEEL SAID HE
may i feel said he
(i'll squeal said she
just once said he)
it's fun said she

(may i touch said he
how much said she
a lot said he)
why not said she

(let's go said he
not too far said she
what's too far said he
where you are said she)

may i stay said he
(which way said she
like this said he
if you kiss said she

may i move said he
is it love said she)
if you're willing said he
(but you're killing said she

but it's life said he
but your wife said she
now said he)
ow said she

(tiptop said he
don't stop said she
oh no said he)
go slow said she

(cccome? said he
ummm said she)
you're divine! said he
(you are Mine said she)
E E CUMMINGS 1935

60

After seeing her act one evening, the Prince de Joinville sent
Rachel Félix his card with the bold invitation: 'Where? - When? -
How much?' and was delighted by her reply:
'Your place - Tonight - Free'.

Prince de Joinville to Rachel Félix and her reply c1840

TAKE HIM

LINDA

Take him, you don't have to pay for him,
Take him, he's free.
Take him, I won't make a play for him,
He's not for me.
True that his head is like lumber,
True that his heart is like ice:
You'll find this little number
Cheap at half the price.

Take him, and just for the lure of it
Marry him too.
Keep him for you can be sure of it,
He can't keep you.
So take my old jalopy,
Keep him from falling apart.
Take him, but don't ever take him to heart.

VERA

Thanks, Little Mousie,
For the present and all that,
But in this housie
I would rather keep a rat.
Only a wizard
Could reform that class of male:
They say a lizard
Cannot change his scale.

61

LINDA

Take him, I won't put a price on him,
Take him, he's yours.
Take him, pyjamas look nice on him,
But how he snores.
Though he is well-adjusted,
Certain things make him a wreck:
Last year his arm was busted,
Reaching from a check.

His thoughts are seldom consecutive,
He just can't write.
I know a movie executive
Who's twice as bright.
Lots of good luck, you'll need it,
And you'll need aspirin too,
Take him, but don't ever let him take you.

DUET

I hope that things will go well with him,
I bear no hate.
All I can say is: - 'To hell with him,
He gets the gate.'
So take my benediction
Take my old Benedict too.
Take him away, he's too good to be true.
LORENZ HART 1952

AGONIES AND LESSONS OF LOVE

HER ANXIETY

Earth in beauty dressed
Awaits returning spring.
All true love must die,
Alter at the best
Into some lesser thing.
Prove that I lie.

Such body lovers have,
Such exacting breath.
That they touch or sigh.
Every touch they give,
Love is nearer death.
Prove that I lie.
W B Yeats 1865-1939

TOURIST

I'm a tourist in the streets of your heart.
I could get lost because the roads are so dark.
I don't know my way and the signs aren't clear
And I can't really speak the language here
Some things cannot be known
Before I go home.

There are footsteps running down every street
But when I look all the ghosts hide and seek
I hear them whisper in broken threads
Are they alive or are they dead
Some things cannot be shown
Before I go back home.
Phantoms cry
And you will always listen to them
Screaming down the past
How can I
Compete with such a chorus?
Their voices break hearts like window glass.

I'm a songbird, the travelling kind.
I move around so I'm quite hard to find
All the houses here look like fairy tales
They're so beautiful but they're not for sale.
Some things cannot be owned
I'm going home.
Sylvie Lewis 1999

LA BELLE DAME SANS MERCI

O, what can ail thee, knight at arms,
Alone and palely loitering:
The sedge has withered from the lake,
And no birds sing.

O, what can ail thee, knight at arms,
So haggard and so woe-begone?
The squirrel's granary is full,
And the harvest's done.

I see a lily on thy brow
With anguish moist and fever-dew,
And on thy cheeks a fading rose
Fast withereth too.

I met a lady in the meads,
Full beautiful - a faery's child,
Her hair was long, her foot was light,
And her eyes were wild.

I made a garland for her head,
And bracelets too, and fragrant zone,
She looked at me as she did love,
And made sweet moan.

I set her on my pacing steed
And nothing else saw all day long;
For sideways would she lean, and sing
A faery's song.

She found me roots of relish sweet,
And honey wild and manna dew;
And sure in language strange she said -
I love thee true.

She took me to her elfin grot,
And there she gazed and sighed full sore:
And there I shut her wild, wild eyes
With kisses four.

And there she lullèd me asleep,
And there I dreamed, ah woe betide,
The latest dream I ever dreamed
On the cold hill side.

I saw pale kings and princes too,
Pale warriors, death-pale were they all:
They cry'd - 'La belle Dame sans Merci
Hath thee in thrall!'

I saw their starved lips in the gloam
With horrid warning gapèd wide,
And I awoke, and found me here
On the cold hill side.

And this is why I sojourn here
Alone and palely loitering,
Though the sedge is withered from the lake,
And no birds sing.

JOHN KEATS 1819

When I was one-and-twenty
I heard a wise man say,
'Give crowns and pounds and guineas
But not your heart away;
Give pearls away and rubies
But keep your fancy free.'
But I was one-and-twenty,
No use to talk to me.

When I was one-and-twenty
I heard him say again,
'The heart out of the bosom
Was never given in vain;
'Tis paid with sighs a plenty
And sold for endless rue.'
And I am two-and-twenty,
And oh, 'tis true, 'tis true.
A E HOUSMAN 1859-1936

NEVER GIVE ALL THE HEART

Never give all the heart, for love
Will hardly seem worth thinking of
To passionate women if it seem
Certain, and they never dream
That it fades out from kiss to kiss;
For everything that's lovely is
But a brief, dreamy, kind delight,
O never give the heart outright,
For they, for all smooth lips can say,
Have given their hearts up to the play.
And who could play it well enough
If deaf and dumb and blind with love?
He that made this knows all the cost,
For he gave all his heart and lost.
W B YEATS 1906

MIRAGE

The hope I dreamed of was a dream,
Was but a dream; and now I wake,
Exceeding comfortless, and worn, and old,
For a dream's sake.

I hang my harp upon a tree,
A weeping willow in a lake;
I hang my silenced harp there, wrung and snapt
For a dream's sake.

Lie still, lie still, my breaking heart;
My silent heart, lie still and break:
Life, and the world, and mine own self, are changed
For a dream's sake.
CHRISTINA ROSSETTI 1830-94

SUMMER SONGS

IT IS THE SWALLOW

It is the swallow,
On whose wing
Yearly the pale
Enchanter, Spring,
Travels with charm
And blossoming spell
To work his usual
Miracle.
He lights the thorn
With stars, and sets
On trees their leafy
Coronets,
While almond bloom
Ensnares the sky
To blue, untranquil
Ecstasy.
He soothes wet woods
With green, and those
Frailer flowers
Than the snows,
Anemones,
And gilds the hill
With cowslip and
With daffodil,
Warming the earth
And warming air
With sun and bird-song
Lovelier

Than tropic countries
Comprehend
Who knew no winter
In their land.
And when the fragrant
Work is done,
And the year set
In motion;
When Summer answers,
With her sweet
Graces, the question
In Spring's heart,
Ah, then by tree
And moon the spell
Winds. Then the happy
Nightingale
Sings for his mate
A dreaming tune,
Cooler than night,
More gold than noon;
And roses open
In the wood,
Where Spring surrendered,
And was glad.
VIOLA GARVIN 1898-

SUMMER

Winter is cold-hearted,
Spring is yea and nay,
Autumn is a weathercock
Blown every way.
Summer days for me
When every leaf is on its tree;

When Robin's not a beggar,
And Jenny Wren's a bride,
And larks hang singing, singing, singing
Over the wheat-fields wide,
And anchored lilies ride,
And the pendulum spider
Swings from side to side.

And blue-black beetles transact business,
And gnats fly in a host,
And furry caterpillars hasten
That no time be lost,
And moths grow fat and thrive,
And ladybirds arrive.

Before green apples blush,
Before green nuts embrown,
Why, one day in the country
Is worth one month in town;
Is worth a day and a year
Of the dusty, musty, lag-last fashion
that days drone elsewhere.
CHRISTINA ROSSETTI 1830-94

SUMMER'S FALL

A November echo when days are lit
the Indian Summer - dead Summer's ghost -
glows, foreshadowing the resurrection.

Having learned for the first time the value
of her charm, she blushes peaches and leaves
Lovers and flowers, pulling their petals
down onto her bed, stretching sleepily
in auburn curves she breathes fruit laden breezes
lingering in the golden gleam and
softly humming incarnadine she melts.

No one dies as beautifully as Summer.
SYLVIE LEWIS 1999

Summer was also the time of these: of sudden plenty, of slow hours and actions, of diamond haze and dust on the eyes, of the valley in post-vernal splendour ... of Mother sleeping heavily at noon; of jazzing wasps and dragonflies, haystooks and thistle-seeds, snows of white butterflies, skylarks' eggs, bee-orchids and frantic ants; of wolf-cub parades, and boy scouts' bugles; of sweat running down the legs; of boiling potatoes on bramble wires, of flames glass-blue in the sun; of lying naked in the hill-cold stream; begging pennies for a bottle of pop; of girls' bare arms and unripe cherries, green apples and liquid walnuts; of fights and falls and new-scabbed knees, sobbing pursuits and flights; of picnics high up in the crumbling quarries, of butter running like oil, of sunstroke, fever, and cucumber peel stuck cool to one's burning brow. LAURIE LEE 1959

ONE TUESDAY IN SUMMER

That sultry afternoon the world went strange.
Under a violet and leaden bruise
The air was filled with sinister yellow light;
Trees, houses, grass took on unnatural hues.

Thunder rolled near. The intensity grew and grew
Like doom itself with lightnings on its face.
And Mr Pitt, the grocer's order-man,
Who made his call on Tuesdays at our place,

Said to my mother, looking at the sky,
'You'd think the ending of the world had come.'
A leathern little man, with bicycle-clips
Around his ankles, doing our weekly sum.
He too looked strange in that uncanny light:

As in the Bible ordinary men
Turn out to be angelic messengers,
Pronouncing the Lord's judgments why and when.

I watched the scurry of the small black ants
That sensed the storm. What Mr Pitt had said
I didn't quite believe, or disbelieve;
But still the words had got into my head.
For nothing less seemed worthy of the scene.
The darkening imminence hung on and on.
Till suddenly, with lightning-stroke and rain.
Apocalypse exploded, and was gone.

By nightfall things had their familiar look.
But I had seen the world stand in dismay
Under the aspect of another meaning
That rain or time would hardly wash away.
JAMES MCAULEY 1917-76

HOME AND HARMONY

THE OWL AND THE PUSSY-CAT
The Owl and the Pussy-cat went to sea
In a beautiful pea-green boat.
They took some honey, and plenty of money,
Wrapped up in a five-pound note.
The Owl looked up to the stars above.
And sang to a small guitar.

'O lovely Pussy! O Pussy, my love,
What a beautiful Pussy you are.
You are,
You are!
What a beautiful Pussy you are!'

Pussy said to the Owl, 'You elegant fowl!
How charmingly sweet you sing!
O let us be married! too long we have tarried:
But what shall we do for a ring?'
They sailed away, for a year and a day,
To the land where the Bong-tree grows
And there in a wood a Piggy-wig stood
With a ring at the end of his nose,
His nose,
His nose,
With a ring at the end of his nose.

'Dear Pig, are you willing to sell for one shilling
Your ring?' Said the Piggy, 'I will.'
So they took it away, and were married next day
By the Turkey who lives on the hill.
They dined on mince, and slices of quince,
Which they ate with a runcible spoon;
And hand in hand, on the edge of the sand,
They danced by the light of the moon,
The moon,
The moon,
They danced by the light of the moon.
Edward Lear 1871

I will make you brooches and toys for your delight
Of bird-song at morning and star-shine at night.
I will make a palace fit for you and me
Of green days in forests and blue days at sea.
I will make my kitchen, and you shall keep your room,
Where white flows the river and bright blows the broom,
And you shall wash your linen and keep your body white
In rainfall at morning and dewfall at night.
ROBERT LOUIS STEVENSON 1896

AN OLD WOMAN OF THE ROADS
O, to have a little house!
To own the hearth and stool and all!
The heaped-up sods upon the fire,
The pile of turf against the wall!

To have a clock with weights and chains
And pendulum swinging up and down,
A dresser filled with shining delph,
Speckled and white and blue and brown!

I could be busy all the day
Clearing and sweeping hearth and floor,
And fixing on their shelf again
My white and blue and speckled store!

I could be quiet there at night
Beside the fire and by myself,
Sure of a bed and loth to leave
The ticking clock and shining delph!
PADRAIC COLUM 1881-1972

When day dawned (for we did not sleep much) and I beheld that beautiful angelic face by my side, it was more than I can express! He does look so beautiful in his shirt only, with his beautiful throat seen. We got up at quarter past 8. When I had laced I went to dearest Albert's room, and we breakfast together. He had a black velvet jacket on, without any neckcloth on, and looked more beautiful than it is possible for me to say .... At 12 I walked out with my precious Angel, all alone - so delightful, on the Terrace and new Walk, arm in arm! Eos our only companion. We talked a great deal together. We came home at one, and had luncheon soon after. Poor dear Albert felt sick and uncomfortable, and lay down in my room .... He looked so dear, lying there and dozing.
QUEEN VICTORIA 1840

FOLDING THE SHEETS
You and I will fold the sheets
Advancing towards each other
From Burma, from Lapland.

From India where the sheets have been washed in the river
And pounded upon stones:
Together we will match the corners.

From China where women on either side of the river
Have washed their pale cloth in the White Stone Shallows
'Under the shining moon'.

We meet as though in the formal steps of a dance
To fold the sheets together, put them to air
In wind, in sun over bushes, or by the fire.

We stretch and pull from one side and then the other -
Your turn. Now mine.
We fold them and put them away until they are needed.

A wish for all people when they lie down in bed -
Smooth linen, cool cotton, the fragrance and stir of herbs
And the faint but perceptible scent of sweet clear water.
ROSEMARY DOBSON 1984

BREAKING UP - THE SADDEST TIME

ONE ART
The art of losing isn't hard to master;
so many things seemed filled with the intent
to be lost that their loss is no disaster.

Lose something every day. Accept the fluster
of lost door keys, the hour badly spent.
The art of losing isn't hard to master.

Then practice losing farther, losing faster:
places, and names, and where it was you meant
to travel. None of these will bring disaster.

I lost my mother's watch. And look! my last, or
next-to-last, of three loved houses went.
The art of losing isn't hard to master.

I lost two cities, lovely ones. And, vaster,
some realms I owned, two rivers, a continent.
I miss them, but it wasn't a disaster.

Even losing you (the joking voice, a gesture
I love) I shan't have lied. It's evident
the art of losing's not too hard to master
though it may look like (Write it!) like disaster.
ELIZABETH BISHOP 1911-79

ON MONSIEUR'S DEPARTURE

I grieve and dare not show my discontent.
I love and yet am forced to seem to hate.
I do, yet dare not say I ever meant.
I seem stark mute yet inwardly do prate.
⠀⠀⠀⠀I am and not, I freeze and yet am burned.
⠀⠀⠀⠀Since from myself my other self I turned.

My care is like my shadow in the sun.
Follows me flying, flies when I pursue it.
Stands and lies by me, doth what I have done.
His too familiar care doth make me rue it.
⠀⠀⠀⠀No means I find to rid him from my breast.
⠀⠀⠀⠀Till by the end of things it be supprest.

Some gentler passions slide into my mind.
For I am soft and made of melting snow:
Or be more cruel, love, and so be kind.
Let me or float or sink, be high or low.
⠀⠀⠀⠀Or let me live with some more sweet content.
⠀⠀⠀⠀Or die and so forget what love ere meant.
QUEEN ELIZABETH I 1582

I was now expecting soon to be called upon to undergo the most fearful ordeal that any woman can possibly be required to pass through - that of giving my husband another wife. The thought of doing this was even worse than death. It would have been fearful to have followed my husband to his grave; but to live and see him the husband of another woman seemed to me like exacting more than human nature was capable of enduring. With all my faith in Mormonism, doubts would arise, and in my bitterest moments of anguish I would exclaim, 'This is more like the work of cruel man than of God. Why should man have this power over woman, and she so helpless? Surely, a just and impartial God can have nothing to do with this!' Then, again, I would come to the conclusion, as I had many times before, that 'the ways of the Lord are past finding out', and, therefore, I must submit.

As the time approached for me to do this, I felt like a condemned felon in his cell, waiting in agony the day of his execution. I knew that my husband suffered also, now that it was so near; for he necessarily saw that it would make a great change in his future life. His freedom was gone.

The dreaded day at length arrived. As may well be supposed, I had passed a very wakeful and unhappy night, and I felt very sick and nervous; for I was soon to become a mother, and it seemed to me that I had not courage to go through that day. However, I nerved myself to the task, and silently made my preparations for going to the 'Endowment House'. The morning was bright and lovely, and calculated to inspire joyous hopes and happy feelings. To me it brought nothing but fear and trembling. I could not even trust myself to speak to my children, for I was choking with suppressed emotion; and they, not knowing how deeply I was suffering, looked at me with wonder in their innocent eyes. 'Oh!' I thought, 'surely my husband will at last understand the depth of the love I bear him; for, were it not that he believes the doctrine to be true, I would even now dash this bitter cup from my lips!' There was a darkness before my eyes, and struggle as I might, I could see no ray of light, no glimmering of hope. I was utterly cast down and broken-hearted, and felt almost as if the Lord had forsaken me. I could not go to my husband for sympathy; for I felt that his thoughts were with his young bride, and that my sorrows would only worry him at a time when he must desire to be at peace.

The time at length arrived for us to go to the 'Endowment House', and there at the altar the first wife is expected to give proof of her faith in her religion by placing the hand of the new wife in that of her husband. She is asked the question by Brigham Young, 'Are you willing to give this woman to your husband, to be his lawful and wedded wife, for time and for all eternity? If you are, you will manifest it by placing her right hand within the right hand of your husband.' I did so. But what words can describe my feelings? The anguish of a whole lifetime was crowded into that one single moment. When it was done, I felt that I had laid everything upon the altar, and that there was no more to sacrifice. I had given away my husband. What more could the Lord require of me that I could not do? Nothing!

I was bewildered and almost beside myself, and yet I had to hide my feelings; for to whom should I turn for sympathy among those who were around me? My husband was there, it is true; but he was now the husband of another woman, and a newly-made bridegroom. I felt that I stood alone, our union was severed. I had given away my husband, and he no longer belonged only to me!
MRS T B H STENHOUSE 1872

False though she be to me and love,
    I'll ne'er pursue revenge;
For still the charmer I approve,
    Though I deplore her change.
In hours of bliss we oft have met;
    They could not always last:
And though the present I regret,
    I'm grateful for the past.
WILLIAM CONGREVE 1670-1729

Oh, when I was in love with you,
Then I was clean and brave,
And miles around the wonder grew
How well did I behave.

And now the fancy passes by
And nothing will remain,
And miles around they'll say that I
Am quite myself again.
A E HOUSMAN 1859-1936

In former days we'd both agree
That you were me, and I was you.
What has now happened to us two,
That you are you, and I am me?
BHARTRHARI 7TH CENTURY

DYING BEFORE TIME

AFTER BLENHEIM

It was a summer evening.
Old Kaspar's work was done,
And he before his cottage door
Was sitting in the sun;
And by him sported on the green
His little grandchild Wilhelmine.

She saw her brother Peterkin
Roll something large and round
Which he beside the rivulet
In playing there had found:
He came to ask what he had found
That was so large and smooth and round.

Old Kaspar took it from the boy
Who stood expectant by;
And then the old man shook his head,
And with a natural sigh
''Tis some poor fellow's skull,' said he,
'Who fell in the great victory.

I find them in the garden.
For there's many here about.
And often when I go to plough
The ploughshare turns them out.
For many thousand men,' said he
'Were slain in that great victory.'

'Now tell us what 'twas all about,'
Young Peterkin he cries;
And little Wilhelmine looks up
With wonder-waiting eyes:
'Now tell us all about the war,
And what they fought each other for.'

'It was the English,' Kaspar cried,
'Who put the French to rout;
But what they fought each other for
I could not well make out.
But everybody said,' quoth he,
'That 'twas a famous victory.

My father lived at Blenheim then,
Yon little stream hard by;
They burnt his dwelling to the ground,
And he was forced to fly:
So with his wife and child he fled,
Nor had he where to rest his head.

With fire and sword the country round
Was wasted far and wide.
And many a childing mother then
And newborn baby died:
But things like that, you know, must be
At every famous victory.

They say it was a shocking sight
After the field was won;
For many thousand bodies here
Lay rotting in the sun:
But things like that, you know, must be
After a famous victory.

Great praise the Duke of Marlbro' won.
And our good Prince Eugene.'
'Why 'twas a very wicked thing!'
Said little Wilhelmine.
'Nay ... nay ... my little girl,' quoth he.
'It was a famous victory.

And everybody praised the Duke
Who this great fight did win.'
'But what good came of it at last?'
Quoth little Peterkin.
'Why that I cannot tell,' said he
'But 'twas a famous victory.'

ROBERT SOUTHEY 1798

ANTHEM FOR DOOMED YOUTH

What passing-bells for these who die as cattle?
Only the monstrous anger of the guns.
Only the stuttering rifles' rapid rattle
Can patter out their hasty orisons.
No mockeries now for them, no prayers nor bells;
Nor any voice of mourning save the choirs, -
The shrill demented choirs of wailing shells;
And bugles calling them from sad shires
What candles may be held to speed them all?
Not in the hands of boys, but in their eyes
Shall shine the holy glimmers of goodbyes.
The pallor of girls' brows shall be their pall;
Their flowers the tenderness of patient minds,
And each slow dusk a drawing-down of blinds.
WILFRED OWEN 1893-1918

On a fine evening during the spring of 1912 I prepared myself happily and confidently for a descent from my solo balloon at the Alexandra Palace. As usual I strolled amongst the spectators as the balloon was being inflated, enjoying my conversations with the people, answering their questions and warmed as always by their friendliness. When the time came, I changed into my parachuting outfit, returned to the enclosure and checked my 'chute as carefully as ever. As I waited for the captain to complete his final preparation of the balloon, I looked up into the sky. There were no clouds. No noisy aeroplanes, either! I would have all that blue space to myself. I was looking forward to it.

The captain indicated that all was ready. I took up my position astride the sling and tightened my grip on the trapeze bar. The crowd grew silent. All eyes were on me.

'LET GO!' I cried.

As the balloon rose, I timed my short run forward so that I was lifted into the air with scarcely a swing. I smiled down on the receding sea of faces and waved my Union Jack in response to their cheers as I soared out over the twin towers of the Palace, upwards and ever upwards, with the noise and the faces of the crowd, and the grounds of the 'Ally Pally' itself dwindling, dwindling .... From my gently swaying perch in space, alone in my silence, I looked down on the well-known and much-loved landscape: Wood Green ... Hornsey ... Southgate ... a patchwork of familiar and friendly faces. I was very much at peace with the world.

The silence of the sky was suddenly broken. It was a voice. I did not imagine it. It spoke once, quite clearly, then no more.

'Don't come up again, or you'll be killed,' it said.

It was quite plain. Just once, it spoke, then left the words echoing in my mind.

'Don't come up again, or you'll be killed.'

I looked around me. The sky was empty. I remained quite still, and very calm, swinging there gently in the silence that had returned. I looked down again at the earth below. It was so beautiful. So remote. So peaceful.

'All right,' I said out loud to whoever it was who had spoken, then with no emotion and no regret and for the last time ever I reached out for the ripping cord.

Back on the ground, amongst the congratulations of the crowd, I gave my little silk Union Jack to a surprised and delighted admirer, and my cap to another, and my parachute badge to someone else.

'I won't be jumping again,' I told the captain. He didn't believe it. 'Oh yes, you will!' he laughed. But he hadn't heard the voice.

As soon as I was back at Aunty's house, I rolled up my parachute costume and put it in the ragbag. Calmly I told my aunt that my parachuting days were over.

'Thank God!' she said.

I did.

DOLLY SHEPHERD 1984

SLOW DANCE

Have you ever watched kids
on a merry-go-round
Or listened to the rain
slapping on the ground?

Ever followed a butterfly's
erratic flight
Or gazed at the sun into the
fading night?

You better slow down
Don't dance so fast
Time is short
The music won't last

Do you run through each day
on the fly?
When you ask 'How are you?'
Do you hear the reply?

When the day is done
Do you lie in your bed
With the next hundred chores
running through your head?

You better slow down
Don't dance so fast
Time is short
The music won't last

Ever told your child
We'll do it tomorrow
And in your haste,
Not seen his sorrow?

Ever lost touch,
Let a good friendship die
'Cause you never had time
To call and say 'Hi'?

You'd better slow down
Don't dance so fast
Time is short
The music won't last

When you run so fast to get
somewhere
You miss half the fun of getting
there.

When you worry and hurry through
your day,
It is like an unopened gift ...
thrown away .....

Life is not a race.
Do take it slower
Hear the music
Before the song is over.
UNKNOWN TEENAGE GIRL, DYING OF CANCER

The life that I have is all that I have;
And the life that I have is yours.
The love that I have of the life that I have,
Is yours and yours and yours.
A sleep I shall have, a rest I shall have,
Yet death will be but a pause,
For the peace of my years, in the
Long green grass, will be
Yours and yours and yours.
LEO MARKS 1940

AUTUMN

THE CHANGING

MOODS

MATURE LOVE

SONNET FROM THE PORTUGUESE XLIII

How do I love thee? Let me count the ways.

I love thee to the depth and breadth and height

My soul can reach, when feeling out of sight

For the ends of Being and ideal Grace.

I love thee to the level of everyday's

Most quiet need, by sun and candlelight.

I love thee freely, as men strive for Right;
I love thee purely, as they turn from Praise.
I love thee with the passion put to use
In my old griefs, and with my childhood's faith.
I love thee with a love I seemed to lose
With my lost saints, - I love thee with the breadth,
Smiles, tears, of all my life! - and, if God choose,
I shall but love thee better after death.

ELIZABETH BARRETT BROWNING 1806-61

LASTING LOVE

And another thing. Love is a temporary madness, it erupts like volcanoes and then subsides. And when it subsides you have to make a decision. You have to work out whether your roots have so entwined together that it is inconceivable that you should ever part. Because this is what love is. Love is not breathlessness, it is not excitement, it is not the promulgation of promises of eternal passion, it is not the desire to mate every second minute of the day, it is not lying awake at night imagining that he is kissing every cranny of your body. No, don't blush, I am telling you some truths. That is just being "in love", which any fool can do. Love itself is what is left over when being in love has burned away, and this is both an art and a fortunate accident. Your mother and I had it, we had roots that grew towards each other underground, and when all the pretty blossom had fallen from our branches we found that we were one tree and not two. But sometimes the petals fall away and the roots have not entwined. Imagine giving up your home and your people, only to discover after six months, a year, three years, that the trees have had no roots and have fallen over. Imagine the desolation. Imagine the imprisonment.

LOUIS DE BERNIÈRES 1994

REFLECTIONS ON LOVE

There is delicious pleasure in clasping in your arms a woman who has caused you much suffering, who has been your cruel enemy for a long time, and who is still ready to be so.

In France men who have lost their wives are sad, while widows on the contrary are gay and happy. There is therefore no equality in the contract of marriage. STENDHAL 1783-1842

The woman who wins is not the one who runs after, not the one who runs away, but the one who waits.

She decided to tell him in advance if she deceived him. He was happy at her confidence .... Then she told him so often that he died of boredom.

How greatly one needs declarations in love, and how greatly one fears them, as though they used up something that would otherwise survive longer. ELIAS CANETTI 1905-1994

AUTUMN IN NATURE

Fall, leaves, fall; die, flowers, away;
Lengthen night and shorten day;
Every leaf speaks bliss to me
Fluttering from the autumn tree.
I shall smile when wreaths of snow
Blossom where the rose should grow;
I shall sing when night's decay
Ushers in a drearier day.
EMILY BRONTË 1818-48

'It's the battle of life - the turbulence of the sea .... I have been fond of the sea all my life, how wonderful it is, yet how terrible it is. But I often think .... what if it suddenly changed its mind and didn't turn the tide? And came straight on? If it didn't stay and came on and on and on and on and on .... That would be the end of it all.' L S LOWRY 1887-1976

TAKING STOCK

BIRTHDAY THOUGHTS
My 35th birthday. Actually I have lied so much about my age that I forget how old I really am. I think I look 28, and I feel 19.
'CHIPS' CHANNON 1934

My after-forty face felt far more comfortable than anything I lived with previously. Self-confidence was a powerful beauty-potion; I looked better because I felt better. Failure and grief as well as success and love had served me well. Finally, I was tapping into that most hard-won of youth dews; wisdom. NANCY COLLINS

I reach the age of sixty. Until about five years ago I detected no decline at all in physical vigour and felt as young as I did at thirty. In the last five years, however, I am conscious that my physical powers are on the decline. I am getting slightly deaf and the passions of the flesh are spent. Intellectually, I observe no decline in vigour; I can write with the same facility, which is perhaps a fault. But I do not notice that my curiosity, my interest or my powers of enjoyment and amusement have declined at all. What is sad about becoming sixty is that one loses all sense of adventure. HAROLD NICOLSON 1946

Still dissatisfied with myself. Must get into a better method. Alas! What have I done today. Looked into Boswell's Life of Johnson; rode with Anne. Wrote one letter and read a little in Xenophon, Denina and Cicero. But what is this? Here is no progress, no exertion! Must dedicate the morning to labour, to composition: begin on Monday. REV W J TEMPLE 1796

DIARY ENTRY FOR 26 JUNE 1924
I did, I think, nothing. EVELYN WAUGH

What I most dread is that life should slip by unnoticed, like a scene half glimpsed from a railway-carriage window. What I want most is to be always reacting to something in my surroundings, whether a complex of visual sensations, a physical activity like skating or making love, or a concentrated process of thought; but nothing must be passively accepted, everything modified by passing it through my consciousness as a worm does earth. FRANCES PARTRIDGE 1940

I put my talent into my work, I put my genius into my life.
OSCAR WILDE 1854-1900

'You will find as you look back upon your life that the moments when you have really lived are the moments when you did things in a spirit of love.' HENRY DRUMMOND

For I have learned
To look on nature, not as in the hour
Of thoughtless youth; but hearing oftentimes
The still, sad music of humanity,
Nor harsh nor grating, though of ample power
To chasten and subdue. And I have felt
A presence that disturbs me with the joy
Of elevated thoughts; a sense sublime
Of something far more deeply interfused,
Whose dwelling is the light of setting suns,
And the round ocean and the living air,
And the blue sky, and in the mind of man;
A motion and a spirit, that impels
All thinking things, all objects of all thought,
And rolls through all things. Therefore am I still

A lover of the meadows and the woods,
And mountains; and of all that we behold
From this green earth; of all the mighty world
Of eye, and ear, - both what they half create,
And what perceive; well pleased to recognise

In nature and the language of the sense,
The anchor of my purest thoughts, the nurse,
The guide, the guardian of my heart, and soul
Of all my moral being ....
WILLIAM WORDSWORTH 1798

There must be more to life than having everything.
MAURICE SENDAK 1928-

We act as though comfort and luxury were the chief
requirements of life when all we need to make us really happy is
something to be enthusiastic about. ANON

THE DONKEY

When fishes flew and forests walked
And figs grew upon thorn,
Some moment when the moon was blood
Then surely I was born;

With monstrous head and sickening cry
And ears like errant wings,
The devil's walking parody
On all four-footed things.

The tattered outlaw of the earth,
Of ancient crooked will;
Starve, scourge, deride me: I am dumb,
I keep my secret still.

Fools! For I also had my hour;
One far fierce hour and sweet:
There was a shout about my ears,
And palms before my feet.
G K CHESTERTON 1874-1936

Sir, I love the acquaintance of young people; because in the first place, I don't like to think myself growing old. In the next place, young acquaintances must last longer, if they do last; and then, Sir, young men have more virtue than old men; they have more generous sentiments in every respect. I love the young dogs of this age, they have more wit and humour and knowledge of life than we had; but then the dogs are not so good scholars. Sir, in my early years I read very hard. It is a sad reflection but a true one, that I knew almost as much at eighteen as I do now. My judgement, to be sure, was not so good; but, I had all the facts. I remember very well, when I was at Oxford, an old gentleman said to me, 'Young man, ply your book diligently now, and acquire a stock of knowledge; for when years come upon you, you will find that poring upon books will be but an irksome task.' SAMUEL JOHNSON 1764

He has achieved success who has lived well, laughed often, and loved much. ANON

RESOLUTIONS WHEN I COME TO BE OLD

Not to marry a young woman.

Not to keep young company unless they really desire it.

Not to be peevish or morose, or suspicious.

Not to scorn present ways, or wits, or fashions, or men,
or war, etc.

Not to be fond of children, or let them come near me hardly.

Not to tell the same story over and over to the same people.

Not to be covetous.

Not to neglect decency, or cleanliness, for fear of falling
into nastiness.

Not to be over severe with young people, but give allowances
for their youthful follies, and weaknesses.

Not to be influenced by, or give ear to knavish tattling servants,
or others.

Not to be too free of advice, nor trouble any but those that
desire it.

To desire some good friends to inform me which of these
Resolutions I break, or neglect, and wherein; and reform
accordingly.

Not to talk much, nor of myself.

Not to boast of my former beauty, or strength, or favour with
ladies, etc.

Not to hearken to flatteries, nor conceive I can be beloved by a
young woman.

Not to be positive or opiniative.

Not to be set up for observing all these Rules, for fear I should
observe none. JONATHAN SWIFT 1699

WORK AND LEISURE

I lost my father when I was nine, so I had to think about work. In those days families didn't have money and boys hurried to work as early as they could so they could earn something. I thought I would be a harness-maker. There was this saddler's shop, you see, right in front of our cottage and a new plate-glass window had been fixed over the small panes of the old window, so you saw the saddlers at work in the lamplight behind the double window. The scene took my eye. I used to long to be inside the window and working away there with the men. It all looked so peaceful and secure.

When I was 12 and a half, I forced myself to go inside and talk to the owner, Mr Peterson - 'Knacker' Peterson was what this gentleman was called - and I told him how I had watched him at work and how I would like to be like him. He listened and then said, 'Very well, I'll take you on. I will give you sixpence a week.'

I wasn't a bound apprentice. I worked a four-year apprenticeship and then one year as an improver. I worked from seven till seven each day and after I became fourteen I got 1s. a week. The war had just started and there was a lot to do, and soon the old gentleman was giving me eighteen-pence a week. Two saddlers were called up and that left only the foreman and myself, which meant that I had to do man's work.

So my wages rose to 5s. - which wasn't man's money. My mother said, 'Well, you can't help it; you've got to honour the arrangement and put up with it.' It was never a very highly paid job for anybody. A journeyman got £1 a week and the foreman a shilling extra. The old gentleman didn't die a rich man but he had his satisfactions. After you had got a job you thought less about what you were paid for it than you did in perfecting what you had to do. No matter how many times a young craftsman did his work wrong or badly, his boss could afford to say, 'Do that again.' Time was money, but such small money as made no difference. We had to 'honour bargains' - it was a religious law among the tradesmen. The old gentleman used to say, 'Horry, if you bargain to do a job for a price, do you do it for that price - even if it takes longer than you thought and you lose a little money. You'll get the customer's good-will, and you'll also learn a sharp lesson on under-estimating time when you have to make another deal.' We had our customers for life. I will say this for the Suffolk farmers, that if you gave them a good deal, they'd stay by you for always. We lived by loyalty.

We also said that the farmers were bad payers, but that was because they hadn't got the money. They were having a bad time like everybody else. The Scotch farmers who came here in the 1930s were really good payers. They worked harder, farmed better - and paid. Their wives helped them. Too many of the Suffolk farmers' wives were trying to be ladies ....

You don't make much money if you work with your hands. You can't make the turnover. But I have no regrets working so slowly. I began in a world without time.

Looking back, I can see that the arrival of the village bus was one of the first nails in the saddler's coffin. One farmer had a motor-plough, it is true, but he was rich. The bus told me that motors wouldn't always be for the rich. During the early part of the Great War some American tractors arrived - huge big things, nearly as vast as traction engines. We didn't worry too much because they couldn't be used in wet weather. When the farmers started buying self-binders I began to take an interest in canvas belts and I learned how to repair them. After 1929 I concentrated on this canvas work, advertised and got most of the contracts for it in all the surrounding villages. It helped us over the change. Just after the last war the first Massey Harris combine arrived in Akenfield; but, again, it was one of those things you could only use on nice fine days. And you couldn't cut barley with it, only wheat. Now they are everywhere and the horses are quite gone. RONALD BLYTHE 1969

I have never done a part, ever, where it hasn't thrown up some kind of problem that I hadn't thought about, where I haven't thought, 'Crikey, how am I going to do this?' When I was first at the Vic, I used to stand at the side of the stage and watch everything every single night. I think you can never stop learning about the business, because actors are so varied in their ways of working. When I became a director, I suddenly learned a lot more, especially about actors' attitudes towards directors. I must have been terrible to direct, but I am better now because I have more sympathy for the director. There are many things you can teach yourself, but you can't teach yourself to have energy. If you are at all lethargic and get tired easily, don't even think about acting. But some things are instinctive. I mean I only ever wanted to be a designer. I trained as a designer and then quite suddenly, quite dramatically, I thought, 'I don't think I can be a designer.' And I changed, seemingly overnight. I went to Stratford, when I was at school, and saw Lear. There was this extraordinary and wonderful set just like a huge rough saucer on the stage, and the middle of it was a cave and a throne and everything just turned around. I was only used to the curtain going up, the curtain going down and then a change of scene. I was really terribly simple-minded and I thought, 'Oh, this is the kind of theatre I believe in,' but then I thought, 'I don't have the imagination to think that way.' I am better at it now, I have learned from working with a lot of wonderful designers.
DAME JUDI DENCH 1997

In the world of building there are so many variables, there is the potential for so many things to create difficulties. Every building is a one-off. We did a major project which is an ocean-going motor yacht which cruises around the world and does three tours every year, one in the Caribbean, one in the Far East and one in the Mediterranean. It moves at 35 knots, it generates its own electricity - it's a floating hotel, it's a restaurant, it's everything, it's unbelievably complex. Yet against all the odds, with all that new technology, it's an extraordinary success story. On the other hand, I can show you a traditional building with absolutely traditional materials which two years after completion will start to have a problem with water penetration that challenges the best brains in Britain. When you're operating at a scale where you are doing some of the most complex buildings in the world - Hong Kong Airport is the largest construction project in the world at the moment, it is one room under a single roof of 45 acres, it is on an island, on land that was made in three years and this building, which is bigger than Heathrow (which evolved over somewhere between 50 and 60 years) is being created in just three years - that poses problems of logistics, of management, of the way that materials come together, of quality control on a scale which is totally new. There is no parallel, it involves for example the largest glazing contract in history. You can guarantee there are going to be problems. Buildings are designed by people, made by people, lived in by people, and we are all imperfect. SIR NORMAN FOSTER 1997

We got on to the subject of work and discussed his poems, and I said there were an awful lot of lines I couldn't understand.

'Oh,' said Dylan, 'I shouldn't worry too much about that. It's like a walled city with many gates, it doesn't really matter which door you go in by - in fact it doesn't matter a tinker's toss if you don't go in at all.'

He lit another cigarette from the stub of the last one. 'Do you mind if we have another cup of coffee and change the subject? I really can't stand it when people ask me questions about my writing, I'm like those birds that eat their young when they're disturbed. Anyway, poetry is not the most important thing

in life, is it? Frankly, I'd much rather lie in a hot bath sucking boiled sweets and reading Agatha Christie, which is just exactly what I intend to do as soon as I get home.'

I said I enjoyed that too, only with me it was Mars bars and Maldorer. He told me I was a dreadful literary snob and we parted most amicably, after I'd settled the bill. Dylan, it seems, is really terribly nice provided you only see him in the mornings.
JOAN WYNDHAM 1943

LEISURE

What is this life if, full of care,
We have no time to stand and stare.

No time to stand beneath the boughs
And stare as long as sheep or cows.

No time to see, when woods we pass,
Where squirrels hide their nuts in grass.

No time to see, in broad daylight,
Streams full of stars like skies at night.

No time to turn at Beauty's glance,
And watch her feet, how they can dance.

No time to wait till her mouth can
Enrich that smile her eyes began.

A poor life this if, full of care,
We have no time to stand and stare.
W H DAVIES 1871-1940

AN AFRICAN ELEGY

We are the miracles that God made
To taste the bitter fruit of Time.
We are precious.
And one day our suffering
Will turn into the wonders of the earth.

There are things that burn me now
Which turn golden when I am happy.
Did you see the mystery of our pain?
That we bear poverty
And are able to sing and dream sweet things

And that we never curse the air when it is warm
Or the fruit when it tastes so good
Or the lights that bounce gently on the waters?
We bless things even in our pain.
We bless them in silence.

That is why our music is so sweet.
It makes the air remember.
There are sweet miracles at work
That only Time will bring forth.
I too have heard the dead singing.

And they tell me that
This life is good
They tell me to live it gently
With fire, and always with hope.
There is wonder here

And there is surprise
In everything the unseen moves.
The ocean is full of songs.
The sky is not our enemy.
Destiny is our friend.
BEN OKRI 1997

RANDOM REFLECTIONS

What an arid place this world would be without nostalgia.
ROSEMARY SUTCLIFF

The future is nothing, but the past is myself, my own history, the seed of my present thoughts, the mould of my present disposition. ROBERT LOUIS STEVENSON

We are all capable of evil thoughts, but only very rarely evil deeds: we can all do good deeds, but very few of us can think good thoughts. CESARE PAVESE

You must have a room or a certain hour of the day or so where you do not know what was in the morning paper ... a place where you can simply experience and bring forth what you are, and what you might be .... At first you may find nothing's happening .... But if you have a sacred place and use it, take advantage of it, something will happen. JOSEPH CAMPBELL

Whoever suffers from the malady of being unable to endure any injustice, must never look out of the window, but stay in his room with the door shut. He would also do well, perhaps, to throw away his mirror. J G SEUME

Man is a gregarious animal, and much more so in his mind than in his body. He may like to go alone for a walk, but he hates to stand alone in his opinions. G SANTAYANA

100

Difficult times have helped me to understand better than before how infinitely rich and beautiful life is in every way and that so many things that one goes worrying about are of no importance whatsoever. ISAK DINESEN

It is a funny thing about life: if you refuse to accept anything but the best, you very often get it. SOMERSET MAUGHAM

Think wrongly, if you please, but in all cases think for yourself. DORIS LESSING

In the middle of difficulty lies opportunity. ALBERT EINSTEIN

It is not fair to ask of others what you are not willing to do yourself. ELEANOR ROOSEVELT

Nothing in life is to be feared. It is only to be understood. MARIE CURIE

The mind, like a parachute, functions only when open. ANON

Be wiser than other people if you can; but do not tell them so. ANON

God grant me the serenity to accept the things I cannot change, the courage to change the things I can, and the wisdom to know the difference. Reinhold Niebuhr

There is no limit to what a man can do or where he can go if he doesn't mind who gets the credit. Anon

ACCIDIE

Our sixth contending is with that which the Greeks called ακηδια and which we may describe as tedium or perturbation of heart. It is akin to dejection and especially felt by wandering monks and solitaries, a persistent and obnoxious enemy to such as dwell in the desert, disturbing the monk especially about midday, like a fever mounting at a regular time, and bringing its highest tide of inflammation at definite accustomed hours to the sick soul. And so some of the Fathers declare it to be the demon of noontide which is spoken of in the Ninety-first Psalm.

When this besieges the unhappy mind, it begets aversion from the place, boredom with one's cell, and scorn and contempt for one's brethren, whether they be dwelling with one or some way off, as careless and unspiritually minded persons. Also, towards any work that may be done within the enclosure of our own lair, we become listless and inert. It will not suffer us to stay in our cell, or to attend to our reading: we lament that in all this while, living in the same spot, we have made no progress, we sigh and complain that bereft of sympathetic fellowship we have no spiritual fruit; and bewail ourselves as empty of all spiritual profit, abiding vacant and useless in this place; and we that could guide others and be of value to multitudes have edified no man, enriched no man with our precept and example. We praise other and far distant monasteries, describing them as more helpful to one's progress, more congenial to one's soul's health .... Towards eleven o'clock or midday it induces such lassitude of body and craving for food as one might feel after the exhaustion of a long journey and hard toil, or the postponing of a meal throughout a two or three days' fast. Finally one gazes anxiously here and there, and sighs that no brother of any description is to be seen approaching: one is for ever in and out of one's cell, gazing at the sun as though it were tarrying to its setting: one's mind is an irrational confusion, like the earth befogged in a mist, one is slothful and vacant in every spiritual activity, and no remedy, it seems, can be found for this state of siege than a visit from some brother, or the solace of sleep.

(FROM THE DESERT FATHERS TRANSLATED BY HELEN WADDELL)

It is not the critic who counts: not the man who points out how the strong man stumbles, or where the doer of deeds could have done them better. The credit belongs to the man who is actually in the arena, whose face is marred by dust, sweat and blood: who strives valiantly; who errs, and comes short again and again, because there is no effort without error and shortcoming; but who does actually strive to do the deeds; who knows the great enthusiasms, the great devotions; who spends himself in a worthy cause; who at the best knows in the end the triumph of high achievement, and who at the worst, if he fails, at least fails while daring greatly, so that his place shall never be with those cold and timid souls who know neither victory nor defeat. THEODORE ROOSEVELT 1858-1919

The future is not some place we are going to, but one we are creating. The paths to it are made not found, and the activity of making them changes both the maker and the destinations. PHILIP ADAMS

FRIENDSHIP

From quiet home and first beginning,
Out to the undiscovered ends,
There's nothing like the wear of winning,
But laughter and the love of friends.
HILAIRE BELLOC 1870-1953

Robert Scott ... was one of my greatest friends at Oxford, but I lost touch with him completely for nearly thirty years. One day I arrived in Nairobi to report the Mau Mau rebellion and forty-eight hours later a message was left at my hotel that the High Commissioner for East Africa wished to see me at his office. He was sending his car and his secretary.

In the car I asked his secretary the High Commissioner's name. 'Sir Robert Scott.' The last time I had heard of Robert he was a Colonial Secretary in Palestine. Scott is a common name. It seemed unlikely that this was my old friend.

'Sir Robert has asked me to show you straight in.'

It was indeed Robert. He sat in the enormous gleaming room completely unchanged, Gaelic, dark, brooding, somehow nervous, behind his great bare desk, fingering a pipe. At Oxford he had always fingered a pipe as though it kept him by a finger's breadth in touch with reality, because the odd thing about this heavy blunt figure, who always seemed to speak with some reluctance, after a long pondering, with a gruff Scottish accent, was that at any moment he was liable to take flight into the irrelevant, irrational world of fantasy.

'Robert!' I exclaimed.

It was as if we had been whirled simultaneously into that Oxford past. At Balliol I had sometimes teased him mercilessly. Coming from a Scottish university, he seemed much older than I was, and his pipe gave him in my eyes an air of bogus wisdom against which I reacted. A puff was the excuse for a long laconic silence. If I hadn't teased him I might have been in danger of accepting him as an authority on life, and that would have been rash indeed.

For instance there had been the affair of the young barmaid of the Lamb and Flag in St Giles whom we all agreed resembled in her strange beauty the Egyptian Queen Nefertiti. What quantities of beer we drank in order to speak a few words with her. We were too young and scared to proceed further, and more than a month of one summer passed before I realised how the slow pipe-smoking wiseacre Robert had succeeded beyond any of us. He was regularly taking her out on her day off in a punt on the Isis and reading her translations from Ronsard. His own translations, for like myself he wrote verse in those days - very traditional verse, but unlike me he was lucky enough not to find a publisher. They might not have done well for his future in the Colonial Office, and anyway who would need a publisher when he had Nefertiti as an audience?

One evening he came to see me. He was even more laconic than usual and puffed a great deal at his pipe. He wanted my advice, he said, and that surprised me, for it had usually been his part to give advice. Apparently Nefertiti had threatened to write to the Dean of Balliol and complain of his conduct.

'What have you done to her?'

'Nothing.'

'Perhaps that's why she's complaining.'

Nevertheless the danger was serious. The Dean, known as 'Sligger', was not a man to sympathise with a heterosexual dilemma. I was at a loss what to advise.

'I have thought of a plan,' Robert said.

'What?'

'I'll invite her to tea, and while she's coming up the stairs I'll lean over the banisters and empty a glass of water on her.'

'But, Robert ... surely that will only make things worse.'

'I can think of nothing else,' he said sadly.

A few weeks later he called on me again. 'It worked,' he said.

'What worked?'

'The glass of water.'

I looked at him in amazement. A douche of cold water ... no more Ronsard ... it seemed to me he must have tapped some deep source of irrational Celtic wisdom. The Lamb and Flag lost a group of customers, but there was no complaint to the Dean.
GRAHAM GREENE 1980

I have had the rarest and most delightful friends. Ah, how I have loved my friends; the rarest wits of my generation were my boon companions; everything conspired to enable me to gratify my body and my brain; and do you think this would have been so if I had been a good man? If you do you are a fool, good intentions and bald greed go to the wall, but subtle selfishness with a dash of unscrupulousness pulls more plums out of life's pie than the seven deadly virtues. If you are a good man you want a bad one to convert; if you are a bad man you want a bad one to go out on the spree with. And you, my dear, my exquisite reader, place your hand upon your heart, tell the truth, remember this is a magical tête-à- tête which will happen never again in your life, admit that you feel just a little interested in my wickedness, admit that if you ever thought you would like to know me that it is because I know a good deal that you probably don't; admit that your mouth waters when you think of rich and various pleasures that fell to my share in happy, delightful Paris; admit that if this book had been an account of the pious books that I had read, the churches I had been to, and the good works I had done, that you would not have bought it or borrowed it. Hypocritical reader, think, had you had courage, health, and money to lead a fast life, would you not have done so? You don't know, no more do I; I have done so, and I regret nothing except that some infernal farmers and miners will not pay me what they owe me and enable me to continue the life that was once mine, and of which I was so bright an ornament. How I hate this atrocious Strand lodging-house, how I long for my apartment in rue de la Tour des Dames, with all its charming adjuncts, palms and pastels, my cat, my python, my friends, blond hair and dark.

GEORGE MOORE 1852-1933

LAUGHTER AND NONSENSE

ON FOOD

Alas! What various tastes in food,
Divide the human brotherhood!
Birds in their little nests agree
With Chinamen, but not with me.
Colonials like their oysters hot,
Their omelettes heavy - I do not.
The French are fond of slugs and frogs,
The Siamese eat puppy-dogs.
The nobles at the brilliant Court
Of Muscovy consumed a sort
Of candles held and eaten thus
As though they were asparagus.

The Spaniard, I have heard it said,
Eats garlic, by itself, on bread:
Now just suppose a friend or dun
Dropped in to lunch at half-past one
And you were jovially to say,
'Here's bread and garlic! Peg away!'
I doubt if you would gain your end
Or soothe the dun, or please the friend.

In Italy the traveller notes
With great disgust the flesh of goats
Appearing on the table d'hôtes;
And even this the natives spoil
By frying it in rancid oil.

In Maryland they charge like sin
For nasty stuff called terrapin;
And when they ask you out to dine
At Washington, instead of wine,
They give you water from the spring
With lumps of ice for flavouring,
That sometimes kill and always freeze
The high plenipotentiaries.

In Massachusetts all the way
From Boston down to Buzzards Bay
They feed you till you want to die
On rhubarb pie and pumpkin pie,
And horrible huckleberry pie,
And when you summon strength to cry,
'What is there else that I can try?'
They stare at you in mild surprise
And serve you other kinds of pies.

And I with these mine eyes have seen
A dreadful stuff called Margarine
Consumed by men in Bethnal Green.
But I myself that here complain
Confess restriction quite in vain.
I feel my native courage fail
To see a Gascon eat a snail;
I dare not ask abroad for tea;
No cannibal can dine with me;
And all the world is torn and rent
By varying views on nutriment.
And yet upon the other hand,
De gustibus non disputand -
- Um.
HILAIRE BELLOC 1870-1953

WHY MR GLADSTONE WORE TROUSERS

The Chancellor of Melbourne University said the other day: 'So long as a man can put his trousers on without sitting down, he is not old.'

The real sign of old age is when you have to lie down to put them on.

With smart men these questions do not arise. Two valets hold the trousers, and the man is lifted up by two other valets, and then slowly lowered into them, as a packing case if lowered by crane into the hold of a ship.

Ruskin used to lie on his bed and raise his legs in the air. Then his man, standing on the bed, used to more or less pour the trousers over his legs. Sometimes they fell too swiftly, and got muddled into a heap above the knee. But it was all one to jolly Jack Ruskin.

Gladstone tried this method once, but the valet got the legs crossed while lowering them. Gladstone said, 'I appear to be squinting somewhat' and sent for an oculist.

The oculist said, 'My dear Prime Minister, do you expect me to make a pair of spectacles for you to wear on your legs?'

'No,' said Gladstone.

'Well then,' said the oculist.

It was only when Gladstone tried to walk that he realised what had happened. He fell over, of course, and hurt his arm. The doctor came, and after examining him said, 'Mr Gladstone, why cannot you put on your trousers like any normal man? If you would only do that, these mistakes would not occur. You might have broken your neck.'

'I might wear knickerbockers, of course,' said Gladstone.

'I don't see that that would make much difference,' said the doctor.

'Knickerbockers have two legs, you know, just as much as trousers.'

'Yes,' said Gladstone, 'but there's less of each leg.'

'I know,' said the doctor, 'but the legs can get crossed, all the same.'

'Then stap me,' said Gladstone, 'I'll stick to trousers.'

And he did. 'BEACHCOMBER' - J B MORTON

THE JOYS OF HUNTING

'Unting is all that's worth living for - all time is lost wot is not spent in 'unting - it is like the hair we breathe - if we have it not we die - it's the sport of kings, the image of war without its guilt, and only five-and-twenty per cent of its danger ....'

... 'Unting fills my thoughts by day, and many a good run I have in my sleep. Many a dig in the ribs I gives Mrs J when I think they're running into the warmint (renewed cheers). No man is fit to be called a sportsman wot doesn't kick his wife out of bed on a haverage once in three weeks!

R S SURTEES 1803-64

I SAW A JOLLY HUNTER

I saw a jolly hunter
With a jolly gun
Walking in the country
In the jolly sun.

In the jolly meadow
Sat a jolly hare.
Saw the jolly hunter.
Took jolly care.

Hunter jolly eager -
Sight of jolly prey.
Forgot gun pointing
Wrong jolly way.

Jolly hunter jolly head
Over heels gone.
Jolly old safety catch
Not jolly on.

Bang went the jolly gun
Hunter jolly dead.
Jolly hare got clean away.
Jolly good, I said.
CHARLES CAUSLEY 1917-

SHEEP

How unconcerned the grazing sheep
Behaving in such manner;
They stand upon their breakfast, they
Lie down upon their dinner.

This would not seem so strange to us
If fish grew round our legs,
If we had floors of marmalade
And beds of buttered eggs.
DOROTHY WELLESLEY

CISSIE PLUMM

Cissie hailed from Bacup, high above Rochdale. She is still remembered for her right to save the Horned Whelk, in Morecambe Bay. Because of man's relentless search for natural gas, silt became disturbed on the ocean bed, and for the whelk which relies on eyesight to find a mate, problems arose. A beachcomber found that half-blinded whelks were trying to mount discarded ice cream cartons at Grange-over-Sands, and in Fleetwood whelks were using shrimps in gang-bangs.

Before long it became apparent that the ecological balance was threatened. Because the Horned Whelk had no nose, it couldn't be fitted with National Health glasses, and nobody knew what to do until Cissie invented small wing mirrors that could be riveted to the ears of the whelk, thus giving the male of the species a chance to get at it, as it were. Today, the Horned Whelk can enjoy life to the full: Cissie organises coach trips for them, and they go to the Lake District to see Kendal Morris Dancers; on the way home, they sing to an accordion and whistle at tins of salmon in the shops. Cissie Plumm was to be given a medal as a tribute from the French Army but they couldn't find a general who would kiss her. LES DAWSON 1983

WINTER

THE PLEASURE

& THE PARTING

AGEING

A benevolent providence mercifully allows everything to deteriorate during one man's lifetime. The summers get worse, the music noisier and more senseless, the buildings uglier, the roads more congested, the trains slower and dirtier, governments sillier and the news more depressing.

Good things, glow-worms, barn owls, farmland, fish shops and girls who enjoyed being called beautiful, were slowly withdrawn.

The process is no doubt a merciful one, because when he comes to the end of his allotted span in a world so remote from the one he had grown up in, the average citizen is quite glad to go. JOHN MORTIMER 1923-

I'M FINE THANK YOU

There is nothing the matter with me,
I'm as healthy as I can be,
I have arthritis in both me knees,
And when I talk I talk with a wheeze.
My pulse is weak and my blood is thin,
But I'm awfully well for the shape I'm in.

Arch supports I have for my feet,
Or I wouldn't be able to be on the street,
Sleep is denied me, night after night,
But every morning I find I'm all right,
My memory is failing, my head's in a spin,
But I'm awfully well for the shape I'm in.

The moral is this as my tale I unfold,
That for you and me who are growing old,
It's better to say 'I'm fine' with a grin,
Than to let folks know the shape we are in.

How do I know that my youth is all spent?
Well, my 'get up and go' has got up and went!
But I really don't mind when I think with a grin,
Of all the grand places my 'get up' has bin!

Old age is golden I've heard it said,
But sometimes I wonder as I get into bed,
With my ears in a drawer and my teeth in a cup,

My eyes on the table until I wake up.
Ere sleep overtakes me I say to myself
Is there anything else I can lay on the shelf?

When I was young my slippers were red,
I could kick my heels over my head,
When I was older my slippers were blue
But still I could dance the whole night through.
Now I am old my slippers are black,

I walk to the stores and puff my way back.
I get up each morning and dust off my wits,
And pick up the paper and read the 'obits'.
If my name is still missing I know I'm not dead,
So I have a good breakfast and go back to bed!
ANON

What is more enchanting than the voices of young people when
you can't hear what they say? L P SMITH

And thus ends all that I doubt I shall ever be able to do
with my own eyes in the keeping of my journall, I being
not able to do it any longer, having done now so long
as to undo my eyes almost every time that I take a pen in my
hand; and therefore, whatever comes of it, I must forbear; and
therefore resolve from this time forward to have it kept by my
people in longhand, and must therefore be contented to set
down no more then is fit for them and all the world to know; or
if there be anything (which cannot be much, now my armours to
Deb are past, and my eyes hindering me in almost all other
pleasures), I must endeavour to keep a margin in my book open,
to add here and there a note in shorthand with my own hand.

And so I betake that course which is almost as much as to see myself go into my grave - for which, and all the discomforts that will accompany my being blind, the good God prepare me.
SAMUEL PEPYS'S FINAL ENTRY 1669

To my dentures I'm accustomed,
To my deafness I'm resigned,
I can manage my bi-focals,
But how I miss my mind!
JOHN HODGE

I don't like getting old; everything about it is horrible. You don't get wiser, well perhaps a little. You get slightly deaf, go a bit lame and don't see as well as you could.
DAME PEGGY ASHCROFT 1907-1989

Life is merely froth and bubble
Two things stand like stone:
Kindness in another's trouble,
Courage in our own.
ANON

Having entered the fiftieth year of my reign and my Jubilee year, I was upset at the thought of those no longer with me, who would have been so pleased and happy, in particular my beloved husband, to whom I owe everything, who are gone to a happier world.

There were beautiful and most kind articles in *The Times*, *Standard* and *St James's*. I don't want or like flattery, but I am very thankful and encouraged by these marks of affection and appreciation of my efforts. QUEEN VICTORIA 1886

George Pulloxfen was as patient as his father was impetuous, and did all by habit. A well-to-do, elderly man, he lived with no more comfort than when he had set out as a young man. He had a little house and one old general servant and a man to look after his horse, and every year he gave up some activity and found that there was one more food that disagreed with him. A hypochondriac, he passed from winter to summer through a series of woollens that had always to be weighed; for in April or May, or whatever the date was, he had to be sure he carried the exact number of ounces he had carried upon that date since boyhood. He lived in despondency, finding in the most cheerful news reasons of discouragement, and sighing every twenty-second of June over the shortening of the days. Once in later years, when I met him in Dublin sweating in a mid-summer noon, I brought him into the hall of the Kildare Street Library, a cool and shady place, without lightening his spirits; for he but said in a melancholy voice, 'How very cold this place must be in winter-time.' Sometimes when I had pitted my cheerfulness against his gloom over the breakfast-table, maintaining that neither his talent nor his memory nor his health were running to the dregs, he would rout me with the sentence, 'How very old I shall be in twenty years.' W B YEATS 1865-1939

WISHES OF AN ELDERLY MAN

I wish I loved the Human Race;
I wish I loved its silly face;
I wish I liked the way it walks;
I wish I liked the way it talks;
And when I'm introduced to one
I wish I thought What Jolly Fun!
SIR WALTER RALEGH c1552-1618

LOOK CLOSER, SEE ME

What do you see, nurses, what do you see?
Are you thinking when you look at me,
A crabbit old woman, not very wise,
Uncertain of habit with faraway eyes,
Who dribbles her food and makes no reply,
When you say in a loud voice, 'I do wish you'd try.'
Who seems not to notice the things that you do
And forever is losing a stocking or shoe,
Who unresisting or not, let's do as you will
Bathing and feeding, the long day to fill,
Is that what you're thinking, is that what you see?
Then open your eyes, nurse, you're not looking at me.

I'll tell you who I am as I sit here so still,
As I move at your bidding, as I eat at your will.
I'm a small child of ten with father and mother,
Brothers and sisters who love one another.
A young girl of sixteen with wings on her feet
Dreaming that soon now a lover she'll meet.
A bride soon at twenty, my heart gives a leap,
Remembering the vows that I promised to keep;
At twenty-five now, I have young of my own
Who need me to build a secure happy home.
A young woman of thirty, my young now grow fast,

Bound to each other with ties that should last;
At forty my young ones now grown will soon be gone,
But my man stays beside me to see I don't mourn;
At fifty, once more babies play round my feet,
Again we know children, my loved one and me.
Dark eyes are upon me, my husband is dead.
I look to the future, I shudder with dread,
For my young are all busy bearing young of their own,

And I think of the years and the love I have known.

I'm an old woman now and nature is cruel,
'Tis her jest to make old age look like a fool.
The body it crumbles, grace and vigour depart,
There now is a stone where once I had a heart.
But inside this old carcass a young girl still dwells,
And now and again my battered heart swells,
I remember the joys, I remember the pain,
And I'm loving and living life over again.
I think of the years all too few - gone too fast
And accept the stark fact that nothing can last.

So open your eyes, nurses, open and see,
Not a crabbit old woman,
Look closer .... see ME.

<small>FOUND IN THE HOSPITAL LOCKER OF AN ELDERLY WOMAN AFTER HER DEATH</small>

WHAT LIPS MY LIPS HAVE KISSED, AND WHERE, AND WHY

What lips my lips have kissed, and where, and why,
I have forgotten, and what arms have lain
Under my head till morning; but the rain
Is full of ghosts tonight, that tap and sigh
Upon the glass and listen for reply,
And in my heart there stirs a quiet pain
For unremembered lads that not again
Will turn to me at midnight with a cry.
Thus in the winter stands the lonely tree,
Nor knows what birds have vanished one by one.
Yet knows its boughs more silent than before:
I cannot say what loves have come and gone,
I only know that summer sang in me
A little while, that in me sings no more.

EDNA ST VINCENT MILLAY 1923

WINTER IN NATURE

Snow fallen upon the leaves had in the night coined or morselled itself into pyramids like hail. Blade leaves of some bulbous plant, perhaps a small iris, were like delicate little saws, so hagged with frost. It is clear that things are spiked with the frost mainly on one side but why this is and how far different things on the same side at the same time I have not yet found. GERARD MANLEY HOPKINS 1872

This hath been such a severe Winter that the like hath not been known since the Year 1683. In some respects it exceeded that. For tho' the Frost did not last so long as it did at that time, yet there was a much greater and deeper Snow. Indeed, it was the biggest snow that ever I knew: as it was also the severest Frost that ever I had been sensible of. It began on Monday, Dec. 5th, and continued 'till Friday, Febr. 10th following, which is almost ten weeks, before there was an intire Thaw. Indeed, it began to thaw two or three times, but then the Frost soon began again with more violence, and there was withall a very sharp and cold and high Wind for some Days. When it first began to thaw and afterwards to Freeze again, it made the ways extreme slippery and dangerous, and divers bad accidents happened thereupon. THOMAS HEARNE 1716

These two nights past I could not be warm all night. I thought it was only poor Mrs Martin and I from age that were so, but speaking to Charles of it this morning, he said he was shivering with cold the whole night and his feet like ice, and could not sleep for the cold, the cook still worse - she was forced to get up in the night and put on stockings and petticoat. I have lain abed these 2 mornings till 10; my ink froze in the glass on the standish - yesterday two bottles of water, which I keep in my study, frozen and burst the bottles, one of which I gently knocked the glass from the bottle from, and the ice in the bottle, neck and all; one mass of ice, just the shape of the bottle.

JOHN BAKER 1776

OF DEATH AND FUNERALS

BECAUSE I COULD NOT STOP FOR DEATH

Because I could not stop for Death -
He kindly stopped for me -
The Carriage held but just Ourselves -
And Immortality.

We slowly drove - He knew no haste
And I had put away
My labour and my leisure too.
For His Civility -

We passed the School, where Children strove
At Recess - in the Ring -
We passed the Fields of Gazing Grain -
We passed the Setting Sun -
Or rather - He passed Us -
The Dews drew quivering and chill -
For only Gossamer, my Gown -
My Tippet - only Tulle -

We paused before a House that seemed
A Swelling of the Ground -
The Roof was scarcely visible -
The Cornice - in the Ground -

Since then - 'tis Centuries - and yet
Feels shorter than the Day
I first surmised the Horses' Heads
Were toward Eternity -
EMILY DICKINSON C1863

Let us go in; the fog is rising.
EMILY DICKINSON 1886

Now the breathing became very noisy, there seemed even a kind of rowdiness about it, and there were little whimperings. The nurse came again and, this time, looked at the clock, made a note. I touched Kate's arm, for it was clearly the end. The last strugglings of breath were immensely laboured, and all the final debris, air and mucus, rattled in the throat. The whole body stirred - and there was one last, long, loud whimper of panic. I thought it was the most unconscious crying of nerves and brain as their last defences fell, and death made ready to dash in. Kate was very much shocked by it, and talked afterwards of her mother as 'a wounded animal', but the cry seemed to me as mindless as a baby's cry at birth. A protest and gasp from a dying machine from which all real personality, capable of suffering in any conscious sense, had surely vanished .... Surely?

The very last loud puffings of breath came from the mouth only, and suddenly - one couldn't quite see how one knew this - the body that had been able to quiver, to stir, however minutely, had become absolutely incapable of movement; death had happened. But even as tears flowed from Kate's eyes, and death was already completely present, the mouth was forced slightly open by a few last little bubbles of air.

And I thought, as we made our shocked and astonished way home, that I'd never seen anything more beautiful. It had been like nothing so much as an oil lamp going out - the flame shortening and guttering and becoming noisy, as the last licks of oil were drawn up. And I saw very well how it was that people spoke of the spirit departing. There had been the most absolute sense of going that I had ever known ....
EDWARD BLISHEN 1981

Say not in grief that he is no more, but in thankfulness that, he was. ANON

Death is nothing at all .... I have only slipped away into the next room. I am I and you are you. Whatever we were to each other, that we still are. Call me by my old familiar name, speak to me in the easy way which you always used. Put no difference in your tone, wear no forced air of solemnity or sorrow. Laugh as we always laughed at the little jokes we enjoyed together. Play, smile, think of me, pray for me. Let my name be ever the household word that it always was. Let it be spoken without effect, without the trace of a shadow on it. Life means all that it ever meant. It is the same as it ever was; there is absolutely unbroken continuity. What is this death but a negligible accident? Why should I be out of mind because I am out of sight? I am but waiting for you, for an interval, somewhere very near just around the corner .... All is well. HENRY SCOTT HOLLAND 1847-1918

My mother died yesterday at quarter to two. I went round at eleven o'clock and she recognised me for a fleeting moment and said 'dear old darling'. Then she went into a coma. I sat by the bed and held her hand until she gave a pathetic little final gasp and died. I have no complaints and regrets. It was as I always hoped it would be. She was ninety-one years old and I was with her close, close, close until her last breath. Over and over this sensible, wise philosophy I know it to be the saddest moment of my life. Owing to my inability to accept any of the comforting religious fantasies about the hereafter, I have no spurious hopes that we shall meet again on some distant Elysian shore. I know that it is over. Fifty-four years of love and tenderness and crossness and devotion and unswerving loyalty. Without her I could only have achieved a quarter of what I have achieved, not only in terms of success and career, but in terms of personal happiness. We have quarrelled, often violently, over the years, but she has never stood between me and my life, never tried to hold me too tightly, always let me go free. For a woman with her strength of character this was truly remarkable. She was gay, even to the last I believe, gallant certainly. There was no fear in her except for me. She was a great woman to whom I owe the whole of my life. I shall never be without her in my deep mind, but I shall never see her again. Goodbye, my darling. Noël Coward 1954

How depressed I felt yesterday evening. How I hung upon the past, as if my life as well as happiness were in it! How I thought of those words 'You will never find another person who will love you as I love you' - And how I felt that to hear again the sound of those beloved, those ever ever beloved lips, I would Barter all other sounds & sights - that I wd. in joy & gratitude lay down before her my tastes and feelings each & all, in sacrifice for the love, the exceeding love which I never, in truth, can find again. Have I not tried this, and know this and felt this: and do I not feel now, bitterly, desolately, that human love like hers [her mother's] I never can find again! Elizabeth Barrett 1831

If I should go before the rest of you,

Break not a flower or inscribe a stone.

Nor when I'm gone speak in a 'Sunday voice',

But be the usual selves that I have known.

Weep, if you must,

Parting is Hell,

But life goes on

So smile as well.

JOYCE GRENFELL 1910-79

The cortège moved on to England. Duff was to be buried at Belvoir but Diana stayed in London. A few months before she had told John Julius that she almost never went to funerals. 'Public ones I grace by official duty, but not the burials of those I love. The idea jars upon me; exhibition of grief, the society duty side does not, in my heart, fit. I do not want to hear the clods fall or be the central tragic figure.'

LADY DIANA COOPER 1892-1986

The very poor are always despised and rebuked because of their fuss and expenditure on funerals. Only today I saw that a public body refused aid to those who had gone any length in such expenditure. Now I do not mean that their crape is my abstract conception of robes of mourning, or that the conversation of Mrs Brown with Mrs Jones over the coffin has the dignity of 'Lycidas'. I do not even say that educated people could not do it better. I say that they are not trying to do it at all. Educated people have got some chilly fad to the effect that making a fuss about death is morbid or vulgar. The educated people are entirely wrong on the fundamental point of human psychology. The uneducated people are entirely right on the point.

The one way to make bereavement tolerable is to make it important. To gather your friends, to have a gloomy festival, to talk, to cry, to praise the dead - all that does change the atmosphere, and carry human nature over the open grave. The nameless torture is to try and treat it as something private and

126

casual, as our elegant stoics do. That is at once pride and pain and hypocrisy. The only way to make less of death is to make more of it. G K CHESTERTON 1874-1936

REMEMBER

Remember me when I am gone away,
Gone far away into the silent land;
When you can no more hold me by the hand,
Nor I half turn to go yet turning stay.
Remember me when no more day by day
You tell me of our future that we planned;
Only remember me; you understand
It will be late to counsel then or pray.
Yet if you should forget me for a while
And afterwards remember, do not grieve:
For if the darkness and corruption leave
A vestige of the thoughts that once I had,
Better by far you should forget and smile
Than that you should remember and be sad.
CHRISTINA ROSSETTI 1830-94

To be deprived of the person we love is happiness compared to living with the one we hate. JEAN DE LA BRUYÈRE 1645-96

LAST POEM

I vow to thee my country - all earthly things above -
Entire and whole and perfect, the service of my love:
The love that asks no questions, the love that stands the test,
That lays upon the altar the dearest and the best;
The love that never falters, the love that pays the price,
The love that makes undaunted the final sacrifice.

And there's another country, I've heard of long ago,
Most dear to them that love her, most great to them that know;
We may not count her armies, we may not see her King;
Her fortress is a faithful heart, her pride is suffering;
And soul by soul and silently her shining bounds increase,
And her ways are ways of gentleness and all her paths are Peace.
SIR CECIL ARTHUR SPRING-RICE 1858-1918

TAKING LEAVE OF LOVED ONES

PARTING

Darling, this is goodbye. The words are ordinary
But love is rare. So let it go tenderly
as the sounds of violins into silence.

Parting is sad for us, because something is over.
But for the thing we have ended, it is a beginning -
Let love go like a young bird flying from the nest.

Like a new star, airborne into the evening,
Watched out of sight, or let fall gently as a tear.
Let our love go out of the world, like the
prayer for a soul's rest ....
KATHLEEN RAINE 1943

LAST LETTER

I only sang love
With the old songs
Touched you with my dreams,
Swung you round
In ripples of laughter,
Wept your silent suffering
In the mute clasp of my hands.

But I never wrote to you.

When you were gone
I raged at frozen fingers
That could not scrape the pen
Across an empty vellum pad;

But you know now
What I could not write to you.
What you could not understand
In my silence
You know now what I was saying.
BARBARA O'HANLON 1999

TWO LIPS

I kissed them in fancy as I came
Away in the morning glow;
I kissed them through the glass of her picture-frame:
She did not know.

I kissed them in love, in troth, in laughter,
When she knew all; long so!
That I should kiss them in a shroud thereafter
She did not know.
THOMAS HARDY 1840-1928

CHRIST

A

MAS

CELEBRATION FOR ALL AGES

Tomorrow, we have to go through all that Christmas business .... It's a funny idea, having a special day for people to be nice to one another. That good will towards men stuff doesn't really work - there's no way of being as generalised as that - you can only feel good will towards those you feel warmly about. You may have it in you to love so very few people when it comes down to it. You want to concentrate real feeling when you have it; you can't disperse it in a fine spray like something out of a garden hose.

H G WELLS 1866-1946

She thought of all the people setting out on journeys they would find exhausting to visit people who were bracing themselves for the disruption of their arrival; and wondered if a moratorium might not be declared every five years during which people would not be allowed to move out of their homes at Christmas! MARY HOCKING

On Boxing Day we did our panto - huge success! I played Aladdin, and had to run on, crying, 'I am that naughty boy Aladdin whose trousers always need some paddin'!' chased by Alfred as the Widow Twankey in a long curly wig, mob-cap and apron, waving a cane! His friend Bertie was divine as the Princess Zadubadour, in a transparent black evening dress, swooning on the floor and murmuring hoarsely, 'Leave me, leave me!' Alfred and Bertie had a great fight over a roll of cotton-wool for their busts. 'Give me my bust, you swine. You can't have it all, damn you!'

Everybody paid sixpence, and we raised 18/- for the Loaves and Fishes. JOAN WYNDHAM 1939

We approached our last house high up on the hill, the place of Joseph the farmer. For him we had chosen a special carol, which was about the other Joseph, so that we always felt that singing it added a spicy cheek to the night. The last stretch of country to reach his farm was perhaps the most difficult of all. In these rough bare lanes, open to all winds, sheep were buried and wagons lost. Huddled together, we tramped in one another's footsteps, powdered snow blew into our screwed-up eyes, the candles burnt low, some blew out altogether, and we talked loudly above the gale.

Crossing, at last, the frozen mill-stream - whose wheel in summer still turned a barren mechanism - we climbed up to

Joseph's farm. Sheltered by trees, warm on its bed of snow, it seemed always to be like this. As always it was late; as always this was our final call. The snow had a fine crust upon it, and the old trees sparkled like tinsel.

We grouped ourselves round the farmhouse porch. The sky cleared, and broad streams of stars ran down over the valley and away to Wales. On Slad's white slopes, seen through the black sticks of its woods, some red lamps still burned in the windows.

Everything was quiet; everywhere there was the faint crackling silence of the winter night. We started singing, and we were all moved by the words and the sudden trueness of our voices. Pure, very clear, and breathless we sang:

> As Joseph was walking
> He heard an angel sing;
> 'This night shall be the birth-time
> Of Christ the Heavenly King.
>
> He neither shall be bornèd
> In Housen nor in hall,
> Nor in a place of paradise
> But in an ox's stall ....'

And two thousand Christmases became real to us then; the houses, the halls, the places of paradise had all been visited; the stars were bright to guide the Kings through the snow; and across the farmyard we could hear the beasts in their stalls. We were given roast apples and hot mince-pies, in our nostrils were spices like myrrh, and in our wooden box, as we headed back for the village, there were golden gifts for all. LAURIE LEE 1959

THE CHRISTMAS ARREST

It was early Christmas morning. I was walking on my beat
When I stopped this man and woman who were loitering in the street.
They had a little baby boy wrapped up in swathing bands
Asleep inside a carry-cot they carried in their hands.

I asked them several questions but their answers were the same:
She called him 'Joseph Carpenter' and 'Mary' was her name.
They did not seem to have a home or other fixed abode.
I took them to the station which was just across the road.

I searched his trouser pockets as required by the law.
I only found a census form and little bits of straw.
I left the woman constable to make a search of her,
And in the baby's carry-cot was frankincense and myrrh.

They said the baby boy was theirs, but called him 'Son of God',
And said they had to hide him here away from one, Herod;
We checked them in the phone book and we searched at CRO,
We fed them in the staff canteen and then we let them go.

I made an entry in my book and went to find the car,
When right above the station yard there shone an eastern star;
Angels on the telephone were ringing up the station,
And written on the message pad was 'Jesus, our Salvation'.
C S PORTEOUS 1988
Solicitor to the Commissioner of Police for the Metropolis at that time

CHRISTMAS

The bells of waiting Advent ring
        The Tortoise stove is lit again
And lamp-oil light across the night
        Has caught the streaks of winter rain
In many a stained-glass window sheen
From Crimson Lake to Hooker's Green.

The holly in the windy hedge
        And round the Manor House the yew
Will soon be stripped to deck the ledge
        The altar, font and arch and pew
So that the villagers can say
'The church looks nice' on Christmas Day.

Provincial public houses blaze
        And Corporation tramcars clang
On lighted tenements I gaze
        Where paper decorations hang
And bunting in the red Town Hall
Says 'Merry Christmas to you all'.

And London shops on Christmas Eve
        Are strung with silver bells and flowers
As hurrying clerks the City leave
        To pigeon-haunted classic towers.
And marbled clouds go scudding by
The many-steepled London sky.

And girls in slacks remember Dad
        And oafish louts remember Mum
And sleepless children's hearts are glad
        And Christmas-morning bells say 'Come!'
Even to shining ones who dwell
Safe in the Dorchester Hotel.

And is it true? And is it true
        This most tremendous tale of all
Seen in a stained-glass window's hue
        A Baby in an ox's stall?
The Maker of the stars and sea
Become a Child on earth for me?

And is it true? For if it is
    No loving fingers tying strings
Around those tissued fripperies
    The sweet and silly Christmas things
Bath salts and inexpensive scent
And hideous tie so kindly meant.

No love that in a family dwells
    No carolling in frosty air
Nor all the steeple-shaking bells
    Can with this single Truth compare
That God was Man in Palestine
And lives to-day in Bread and Wine.

JOHN BETJEMAN 1906-84

CAROLLERS AT MOLE END

It was a pretty sight, and a seasonable one, that met their eyes when they flung the door open. In the fore-court, lit by the dim rays of a horn lantern, some eight or ten little field mice stood in a semicircle, red worsted comforters round their throats, their fore-paws thrust deep into their pockets, their feet jiggling for warmth. With bright beady eyes they glanced shyly at each other, sniggering a little, sniffing and applying coat-sleeves a good deal. As the door opened, one of the elder ones that carried the lantern was just saying, 'Now then, one, two, three!' and forthwith their shrill little voices uprose on the air, singing one of the old-time carols that their forefathers composed in fields that were fallow and held by frost, or when snow-bound in chimney corners, and handed down to be sung in the miry street to lamp-lit windows at Yuletime.

    Villagers all, this frosty tide
    Let your doors swing open wide,
    Though wind may follow, and snow beside,
    Yet draw us in by your fire to bide;
    Joy shall be yours in the morning!

Here we stand in the cold and the sleet,
Blowing fingers and stamping feet,
Come from far away you to greet -
You by the fire and we in the street -
Bidding you joy in the morning!

For ere one half of the night was gone,
Sudden a star has let us on,
Raining bliss and benison -
Bliss to-morrow and more anon,
Joy for every morning!

Goodman Joseph toiled through the snow -
Saw the star o'er a stable low;
Mary she might not further go -
Welcome thatch, and little below!
Joy was hers in the morning!

And then they heard the angels tell
'Who were the first to cry Nowell?
Animals all, as it befell,
In the stable where they did dwell!
Joy shall be theirs in the morning!

The voices ceased, the singers, bashful but smiling, exchanged sidelong glances, and silence succeeded - but for a moment only. Then, from up above and far away, down the tunnel they had so lately travelled was borne, to their ears in a faint musical hum the sound of distant bells ringing a joyous and clangerous peal.

'Very well sung, boys!' cried the Rat heartily, 'and now come along in all of you, and warm yourselves by the fire, and have something hot!' KENNETH GRAHAME 1859-1932

CHRISTMAS TRUCE

I have just been through one of the most extraordinary scenes imaginable. Tonight is Xmas Eve and I came up into the trenches this evening for my tour of duty in them. Firing was going on all the time and the enemy's machine guns were at it hard, firing at us. Then about seven the firing stopped.

I was in my dugout reading a paper and the mail was being dished out. It was reported that the Germans had lighted their trenches up all along our front. We had been calling to one another for some time Xmas wishes and other things. I went out and they shouted 'no shooting' and then somehow the scene became a peaceful one. All our men got out of the trenches and sat on the parapet, the Germans did the same, and they talked to one another in English and broken English. I got on the top of the trench and talked German and asked them to sing a German Volkslied (folk song), which they did, then our men sang quite well and each side clapped and cheered the other.

I asked a German who sang a solo to sing one of Schumann's songs, so he sang 'The Two Grenadiers' splendidly. Our men were a good audience and really enjoyed his singing.

Then Pope and I walked across and held a conversation with the German officer in command. One of his men introduced us properly, he asked my name and then presented me to his officer. I gave the latter permission to bury some German dead who were lying in between us, and we agreed to have no shooting until 12 midnight tomorrow. We talked together, 10 or more Germans gathered round. I was almost in their lines within a yard or so. We saluted each other, he thanked me for permission to bury his dead, and we fixed up how many men were to do it, and that otherwise both sides must remain in their trenches.

Then we wished one another good night and a good night's rest, and a happy Xmas and parted with a salute. I got back to the trench. The Germans sang 'Die Wacht am Rhein', it sounded well. Then our men sang quite well 'Christmas Awake'. It sounded so well, and with a good night we all got back into our trenches. It was a curious scene, a lovely moonlight night, the German trenches with small lights on them, and the men on both sides gathered in groups on the parapets.

At times we heard the guns in the distance and an occasional rifle shot. I can hear them now, but about us is absolute quiet. I allowed one or two men to go out and meet a German or two halfway. They exchanged cigars, and smoked and talked. The officer I spoke to hopes we shall do the same on New Year's Day. I said 'yes, if I am here'. I felt I must sit down and write the story of this Xmas Eve before I went to lie down. Of course no precautions are relaxed, but I think they mean to play the game. All the same, I think I shall be awake all night so as to be on the safe side. It is weird to think that tomorrow night we shall be at it hard again. If one gets through this show it will be a Xmas time to live in one's memory. The German who sang had a really fine voice.

Am just off for a walk round the trenches to see all is well. Good night. CAPTAIN R J ARMES 1917

SCROOGE

Running to the window, he opened it, and put out his head. No fog, no mist; clear, bright, jovial, stirring, cold; cold, piping for the blood to dance to; golden sunlight; heavenly sky; sweet fresh air: merry bells. Oh, glorious. Glorious!

'What's today?' cried Scrooge, calling downward to a boy in Sunday clothes, who perhaps had loitered in to look about him.

'Eh?' returned the boy, with all his might of wonder.

'What's today, my fine fellow?' said Scrooge.

'Today!' replied the boy. 'Why CHRISTMAS DAY.'

'It's Christmas Day!' said Scrooge to himself. 'I haven't missed it. The Spirits have done it all in one night. They can do anything they like. Of course they can. Of course they can. Hallo, my fine fellow!'

'Hallo!' returned the boy.

'Do you know the poulterer's, in the next street but one, at the corner?' Scrooge inquired.

'I should hope I did,' replied the lad.

'An intelligent boy!' said Scrooge. 'A remarkable boy! Do you know whether they've sold the prize Turkey that was hanging up there? Not the little prize Turkey: the big one?'

'What the one as big as me?' returned the boy.

'What a delightful boy!' said Scrooge. 'It's a pleasure to talk to him. Yes. My buck!'

'It's hanging there now,' replied the boy.

'It is?' exclaimed Scrooge, 'I am in earnest. Go and buy it, and tell 'em to bring it here, that I may give them the direction where to take it. Come back with the man, and I'll give you a shilling. Come back with him in less than five minutes, and I'll give you half-a-crown!'

The boy was off like a shot. He must have had a steady hand at a trigger who could have got a shot off half so fast.

'I'll send it to Bob Cratchit's!' whispered Scrooge, rubbing his hands, and splitting with a laugh. 'He shan't know who sends it. It's twice the size of Tiny Tim. Joe Miller never made such a joke as sending it to Bob's will be!'

The hand in which he wrote the address was not a steady one, but write it he did, somehow, and went down stairs to open the street door, ready for the coming of the poulterer's man. As he stood there, waiting his arrival, the knocker caught his eye.

'I shall love it, as long as I live!' cried Scrooge, patting it with his hand. 'I scarcely ever looked at it before. What an honest expression it has in its face! It's a wonderful knocker! - Here's the Turkey. Hallo! Whoop! How are you! Merry Christmas!'

It *was* a Turkey! He could never had stood upon his legs,

that bird. He would have snapped 'em short off in a minute, like sticks of sealing-wax.

'Why, it's impossible to carry that to Camden Town,' said Scrooge. 'You must have a cab.'

The chuckle with which he said this, and the chuckle with which he paid for the turkey, and the chuckle with which he paid for the cab, and the chuckle with which he recompensed the boy, were only to be exceeded by the chuckle with which he sat down breathless in his chair again, and chuckled till he cried.

Shaving was not an easy task, for his hand continued to shake very much; and shaving required attention, even when you don't dance while you are at it. But if he had cut the end of his nose off, he would have put a piece of sticking-plaster over it, and been quite satisfied.

He dressed himself 'all in his best', and at last got out into the streets. The people were by this time pouring forth, as he had seen them with the Ghost of Christmas Present; and walking with his hands behind him, Scrooge regarded everyone with a delighted smile. He looked so irresistibly pleasant, in a word, that three or four good-humoured fellows said, 'Good morning, Sir! A Merry Christmas to you!' and Scrooge said often afterwards, that of all the blithe sounds he had ever heard, those were the blithest in his ears....

At last the dinner was all done, the cloth was clear, the hearth swept, and the fire made up. The compound in the jug being tasted and considered perfect, apples and oranges were put upon the table, and a shovel-full of chestnuts on the fire. Then all the Cratchit family drew round the hearth, in what Bob Cratchit called a circle, meaning half a one; and at Bob Cratchit's elbow, stood the family display of glass; two tumblers, and a custard-cup without a handle.

These held the hot stuff from the jug, however, as well as golden goblets would have done; and Bob served it out with beaming looks, while the chestnuts on the fire sputtered and crackled noisily. Then Bob proposed:

'A Merry Christmas to us all, my dears. God bless us!'
Which all the family re-echoed.

'God bless us every one!' said Tiny Tim, the last of all.

PAUSE

And so, as Tiny Tim observed, God Bless Us, Every One!
CHARLES DICKENS 1843

A CHILD'S CHRISTMAS IN WALES

One Christmas was so much like another, in those years around the sea-town corner now and out of all sound except the distant speaking of the voices I sometimes hear a moment before sleep, that I can never remember whether it snowed for six days and six nights when I was twelve or whether it snowed for twelve days and twelve nights when I was six.

It was on the afternoon of the day of Christmas Eve, and I was in Mrs Prothero's garden, waiting for cats, with her son Jim. It was snowing. It was always snowing at Christmas. December, in my memory, is white as Lapland, there were no reindeers. But there were cats. Patient, cold and callous, our hands wrapped in socks, we waited - to snowball the cats. Sleek and long as jaguars and horrible-whiskered, spitting and snarling, they would slink and sidle over the white back-garden walls; and the lynx-eyed hunters, Jim and I, fur-capped and moccasined trappers from Hudson Bay, off Mumbles Road, would hurl our deadly snowballs at the green of their eyes.

The wise cats never appeared. We were so still, Eskimo-footed arctic marksmen in the muffling silence of the eternal snows - eternal, ever since Wednesday - that we never heard Mrs Prothero's first cry from her igloo at the bottom of the garden. Or, if we heard it at all, it was, to us, like the far-off challenge of our enemy and prey, the neighbour's polar cat. But soon the voice grew louder. 'Fire!' cried Mrs Prothero, and she beat the dinner-gong.

And we ran down the garden, with the snowballs in our arms, toward the house; and smoke, indeed, was pouring out of the dining-room, and the gong was bombilating, and Mrs Prothero was announcing ruin like a town crier in Pompeii. This was better than all the cats in Wales standing on the wall in a row. We bounded into the house, laden with snowballs, and stopped at the open door of the smoke-filled room.

Something was burning all right; perhaps it was Mr Prothero, who always slept there after midday dinner with a newspaper over his face. But he was standing in the middle of the room, saying 'A fine Christmas!' and smacking at the smoke with a slipper. 'Call the fire brigade,' cried Mrs Prothero as she beat the gong.

'They won't be there,' said Mr Prothero, 'it's Christmas.'

There was no fire to be seen, only clouds of smoke and Mr Prothero standing in the middle of them, waving his slipper as though he were conducting.

'Do something,' he said.

And we threw all our snowballs into the smoke - I think we missed Mr Prothero - and ran out of the house to the telephone box.

'Let's call the police as well,' Jim said.

'And the ambulance.'

'And Ernie Jenkins, he likes fires.'

But we only called the fire brigade, and soon the fire engine came and three tall men in helmets brought a hose into the house and Mr Prothero got out just in time before they turned it on. Nobody could have had a noisier Christmas Eve. And when the firemen turned off the hose and were standing in the wet, smoky room, Jim's aunt, Miss Prothero, came downstairs and peered in at them. Jim and I waited, very quietly, to hear what she would say to them. She said the right thing, always. She looked at the three tall firemen in their shining helmets, standing among the smoke and cinders and dissolving snowballs, and she said: 'Would you like anything to read?'

That night we went singing carols, when there wasn't the shaving of a moon to light the flying streets. At the end of a long road was a drive that led to a large house, and we stumbled up the darkness of the drive, each one of us afraid, each one holding a stone in his hand in case, and all of us too brave to say a word. The wind through the trees made noises as of old and unpleasant and maybe webfooted men wheezing in caves. We reached the black bulk of the house.

'What shall we give them? Hark the Herald?'

'No,' Jack said, 'Good King Wenceslas. I'll count three.'

One, two, three, and we began to sing, our voices high and seemingly distant in the snow-felted darkness round the house that was occupied by nobody we knew. We stood close together, near the dark door.

Good King Wenceslas looked out
On the Feast of Stephen ....

And then a small, dry voice, like the voice of someone who has not spoken for a long time, joined our singing: a small, dry, eggshell voice from the other side of the door: a small dry voice through the keyhole. And when we stopped running we were outside our house; the front room was lovely; balloons floated under the hot-water-bottle gulping gas; everything was good again and shone over the town.

'Perhaps it was a ghost,' Jim said.

'Perhaps it was trolls,' Dan said, who was always reading.

'Let's go in and see if there's any jelly left,' Jack said. And we did that.

Always on Christmas night there was music. An uncle played

the fiddle, a cousin sang 'Cherry Ripe', and another uncle sang 'Drake's Drum'. It was very warm in the little house. Auntie Hannah, who had got on to the parsnip wine, sang a song about Bleeding Hearts and Death, and then another in which she said her heart was like a Bird's Nest; and then everybody laughed again; and then I went to bed. Looking through my bedroom window, out into the moonlight and the unending smoke-coloured snow, I could see the lights in the windows of all the other houses on our hill and hear the music rising from them up the long, steadily falling night. I turned the gas down, I got into bed. I said some words to the close and holy darkness, and then I slept.
DYLAN THOMAS 1914-53

WILLIAM'S TRUTHFUL CHRISTMAS

William awoke early on Christmas day. He had hung up his stocking the night before and was pleased to see it fairly full. He took out the presents quickly but not very optimistically. He had been early disillusioned in the matter of grown-ups' capacity for choosing suitable presents. Memories of prayer books and history books and socks and handkerchiefs floated before his mental vision .... Yes, as bad as ever! ... a case containing a pen and pencil and ruler, a new brush and comb, a purse (empty) and a new tie ... a penknife and a box of toffee were the only redeeming features. On the chair by his bedside was a book of Church History from Aunt Emma and a box containing a pair of compasses, a protractor and a set square from Uncle Frederick ....

William dressed, but as it was too early to go down he sat on the floor and ate all his tin of toffee. Then he turned his attention to his deeds of the saintly Aidan which so exasperated him that he was driven to relieve his feeling by taking his new pencil from its case and adorning the saint's picture by the addition of a top hat and spectacles. He completed the

145

alterations by a moustache and by changing the book the saint held into an attaché case. He made similar alterations to every picture in the book .... St Oswald seemed much improved by them and this cheered William considerably. Then he took his penknife and began to carve his initials upon his brush and comb ....

William appeared at breakfast wearing his new tie and having brushed his hair with his new brush or rather what was left of his new brush after his very drastic initial carving. He carried under his arm his presents for his host and hostess. He exchanged 'Happy Christmas' gloomily. His resolve to cast away deceit and hypocrisy and speak the truth with another lay heavy upon him. He regarded it as an obligation that could not be shirked. William was a boy of great tenacity of purpose. Having once made up his mind to a course he pursued it regardless of consequences ....

'Well, William, darling,' said his mother. 'Did you find your presents?'

'Yes,' said William gloomily. 'Thank you.'

'Did you like the book and instruments that Uncle and I gave you?' said Aunt Emma brightly.

'No,' said William gloomily and truthfully. 'I'm not int'rested in Church History an' I've got something like those at school. Not that I'd want 'em,' he added hastily, 'if I hadn't 'em.'

'William!' screamed Mrs Brown in horror. 'How can you be so ungrateful!'

'I'm not ungrateful,' explained William wearily. 'I'm only bein' truthful. I'm casting aside deceit an' ... 'hyp-hyp-what he said. I'm only sayin' that I'm not int'rested in Church History nor in those inst'ments. But thank you very much for 'em.'

There was a gasp of dismay and a horrified silence during which William drew his paper packages from under his arm.

'Here are your Christmas presents from me,' he said.

The atmosphere brightened. They unfastened their parcels

with expressions of anticipation and Christian forgiveness upon their faces.

'It's very kind of you,' said Aunt Emma, still struggling with the string.

'It's not kind,' said William, still treading doggedly the path of truth. 'Mother said I'd got to bring you something.'

Mrs Brown coughed suddenly and loudly but not in time to drown the fatal words of truth ....

'But still-er-very kind,' said Aunt Emma though with less enthusiasm.

At last she brought out a small pincushion.

'Thank you very much,' William, she said. 'You really oughtn't to have spent your money on me like this.'

'I din't,' said William stonily. 'I hadn't any money, but I'm very glad you like it. It was left over from Mother's stall at the Sale of Work, an' Mother said it was no use keepin' it for nex' year because it had got so faded.'

Again Mrs Brown coughed loudly but too late. Aunt Emma said coldly:

'I see. Yes. Your mother was quite right. But thank you all the same, William.'

Uncle Frederick had now taken the wrappings from his present and held up a leather purse.

'Ah, this is a really useful present,' he said jovially.

'I'm 'fraid it's not very useful,' said William. 'Uncle Jim sent it to father for his birthday but father said it was no use 'cause the catch wouldn' catch so he gave it to me to give to you.'

Uncle Frederick tried the catch.

'Um ... ah ....' he said. 'Your father was quite right. The catch won't catch. Never mind, I'll send it back to your father as a New Year present ... what?'

As soon as the Brown family were left alone it turned upon William in a combined attack.

'I warned you!' said Ethel to her mother.

'He ought to be hung,' said Robert.

'William, how could you?' said Mrs Brown.

'When I'm bad, you go on at me,' said William with exasperation, 'an' when I'm tryin' to lead a holier life and cast aside hyp-hyp-what he said, you go on at me. I dunno what I can be. I don't mind bein' hung. I'd as soon be hung as keep havin' Christmas over an' over again simply every year the way we do ....'

Richmal Crompton 1890-1969

ON THE TWELFTH DAY OF CHRISTMAS I SCREAMED

Now April's here, what ever can I do
With those fantastic gifts I got from you?
Spring's in the air, but honey life is hard:
The three French hens are pecking in the yard,
And the turtledove, the turtledove
(One of them died)
Ah, love, my own true love, you have denied
Me nothing the mails or the express could bring
But look: we're into spring;
The calling birds are calling, calling;
The pear tree's leaves are slowly falling;
I sit here with these cackling geese
And never know a moment's peace.
My memories are mixed and hazy
The drumming drummers drive me crazy,
The milking maids enjoy canasta,
The Lords are leaping ever faster.
The pipers - God in Heaven knows
I've more than had enough of those.

My love, you do such wondrous things
(Who else would think of five gold rings?)
I know you send me all you can
Of spoils of occupied Japan.
But you remain on alien shore
And waiting here is such a bore.
My love, the lively lords are leaping
Some things will not improve with keeping....
DAVID DAICHES 1912-

And now let us welcome the New Year
Full of things that have never been.
RAINER MARIA RILKE 1875-1926

ACKNOWLEDGMENTS

The editor and the publisher are grateful to the following for permission to reproduce copyright material:

AP Watt Ltd (on behalf of Michael B Yeats) for 'He Wishes for the Cloths of Heaven', 'Her Anxiety' and 'Never Give All the Heart' by W B Yeats; (on behalf of The Royal Literary Fund) for 'The Donkey' and an extract from *Tommy and the Traditions* by G K Chesterton; and (on behalf of the National Trust for Places of Historic Interest or Natural Beauty) for 'If' by Rudyard Kipling.

Elizabeth Barnett, literary executor for 'I, being born a woman and distressed' and 'What lips my lips have kissed, and where, and why' from *The Collected Poems of Edna St Vincent Millay* (HarperCollins).

Bloomsbury Publishing for an extract from *Off the Rails, Memoirs of a Train Addict* by Lisa St Aubin de Teran.

David Bolt Associates for an extract from *How We Lived Then* by Norman Longmate (Hutchinson).

Carcanet Press Ltd for 'Strawberries' and an extract from 'The Unspoken', both by Edwin Morgan.

Constable & Co for an extract from *The Desert Fathers* translated by Helen Waddell.

Curtis Brown (on behalf of the Estate of Sir Winston S Churchill), for an extract from *My Early Life - A Roving Commission* by Winston S Churchill (copyright Winston S Churchill); and (on behalf of The University Chest, Oxford) for 'Carollers at Mole End' from *Wind in the Willows* by Kenneth Grahame (copyright The University Chest, Oxford).

H M Davies Will Trust for 'Leisure' from *Autobiography of a Supertramp* by W H Davies (Jonathan Cape).

André Deutsch for an extract from *The Human Province* by Elias Canetti.

The Dolmen Press for 'Elizabeth in Italy' from *Stephen's Green Revisited* by Richard Weber.

Gerald Duckworth & Co Ltd for an extract from *Iris: A Memoir* by John Bayley.

Egmont Children's Books for 'Us Two' from *Winnie-the-Pooh* by A A Milne.

Express Newspapers, for 'Why Mr Gladstone Wore Trousers' from *Beachcomber, The Works of J B Morton*

Fabulous Music Ltd for 'Pictures of Lily' by Pete Townshend.

Faber & Faber for 'The Railway Children' from *Station Island* by Seamus Heaney; extract from *Period Piece - A Cambridge Childhood* by Gwen Raverat; extract from *Free Association, an Autobiography* by Steven Berkoff; 'One Tuesday in Summer' by James McAuley and 'Folding the Sheets' by Rosemary Dobson from *The School Bag*; and 'The Trees' from *Collected Poems* by Philip Larkin.

Farrar, Strauss & Giroux Inc for 'One Art' from *Complete Poems, 1927-1979* by Elizabeth Bishop.

David Godwin Associates for an extract from *An African Elegy* by Ben Okri.

Harcourt Brace & Company for 'may I feel said he' in *Complete Poems 1913-1962* by E E Cummings.

HarperCollins Publishers Ltd for *Harold Nicolson: Diaries and Letters* by Harold Nicolson and an extract from *Basingstoke Boy* by John Arlott.

A M Heath for an extract from *Shaky Relations* by Edward Blishen (Hamish Hamilton).

David Higham Associates Ltd for 'A Child's Christmas in Wales' by Dylan Thomas (J M Dent); 'I Saw a Jolly Hunter' from *Collected Poems* by Charles Causley (Macmillan); extract from *Boy - Tales of Childhood* by Roald Dahl (Jonathan Cape); extract from *Ways of Escape* by Graham Greene (Penguin); extract from *The Day Gone By* by Richard Adams (Hutchinson); extract from *Pardon Me For Living* by Geoffrey Green (George Allen & Unwin); and 'On the Twelfth Day of Christmas I Screamed' by David Daiches.

International Music Publications for 'Take Him', words and music by Richard Rodgers and Lorenz Hart © 1981 Warner/Chappell Music Ltd.

Benedicta Leigh for an extract from *The Catch of Hands, An Autobiography* by Benedicta Leigh.

Macmillan Children's Books for 'William's Truthful Christmas' by Richmal Crompton.

John Murray (Publishers) Ltd, for an extract from *Traveller's Prelude* by Freya Stark; 'False Security' from *Summoned by Bells* and 'Christmas' from *Collected Poems* by John Betjeman.

Orion Publishing Group Ltd for extracts from *The Noel Coward Diaries* by Noel Coward; *Clinging to the Wreckage* by John Mortimer; and 'It is the Swallow' from *Dedication* by Viola Garvin.

Maire O'Sullivan for 'An Old Woman of the Roads' by Padraic Colum.

Oxford University Press for an extract from *Lark Rise to Candleford* by Flora Thompson.

Penguin UK for extracts from *Memoirs of a Dutiful Daughter* by Simone de Beauvoir (Penguin) and *Born Lucky* by John Francome (Pelham Books).

Penguin USA for an extract from *Georgia O'Keefe* by Georgia O'Keefe.

Peters Fraser & Dunlop Group Ltd on behalf of the setate of Hilaire Belloc for 'Friendship' and 'On Food' by Hilaire Belloc.

Chris Porteous CBE for 'The Christmas Arrest' by C S Porteous.

Praxis Books for 'Ambitions' from *Petals in the Mind* by Venetia Carse.

Rogers, Coleridge & White for extracts from *A Pacifist's War* by Frances Partridge (Hogarth Press) and *Akenfield* by Ronald Blythe (Allen Lane: The Penguin Press).

Random House Group Ltd for extracts from *Captain Corelli's Mandolin* by Louis De Bernières (Secker & Warburg); *Cider with Rosie* by Laurie Lee (Hogarth Press); *Love Is Blue - a Wartime Diary*, and *Love Lessons* by Joan Wyndham (Heinemann); *The Growing Pains of Adrian Mole* by Sue Townsend (Random House Group Ltd); *Vanessa Redgrave, An Autobiography* by Vanessa Redgrave (Hutchinson); *Memoirs* by Kingsley Amis; *My Last Breath* by Luis Buñuel (Jonathan Cape); and 'Come live with me and be my love', from *The Complete Poems* by C Day Lewis (Sinclair-Stevenson, 1992) copyright © 1992 in this edition and the estate of C Day Lewis).

Mrs Molly Sedgwick for an extract from *When the 'Chute Went Up, The Adventures of a Pioneer Lady Parachutist* by Dolly Shepherd, with Peter Hearn and Molly Sedgwick (second edition, published by Skyline).

Sheil Land for an extract from *Joyce by Herself and Her Friends* by Joyce Grenfell.

Colin Smythe for an extract from *Confessions of a Young Man* by George Moore.

Society of Authors (on behalf of the Estate of A E Housman), for 'Loveliest of trees, the cherry now' and 'When I was one-and-twenty', by A E Housman.

Every effort has been made to trace all copyright holders and the publisher apologises to anyone who has not been found or properly acknowledged. Subsequent editions will include any corrections or omissions notified to the publisher.

AUTHOR'S ACKNOWLEDGMENT

My thanks to my editor Michael Leitch for tracking down the source of many of my favourite pieces and for helping me to assemble this anthology, to David Pocknell and his design team for the elegant typography, to Paul Cooper for the jacket design, to Siân Trenberth for the cover photograph originally taken on the Skirrid mountain for the Wales Tourist Board and reproduced with their kind permission, and to Peggy Atkinson for suggesting some of her own personal favourites which have now become a valued part of my own collection.

To Liz, my literary conscience, with love

EDITOR'S NOTE

A single date after a main contributor's name
refers to the year of writing or the date of first
publication. Where we have been unable to
establish this, we have given the contributor's full
dates wherever possible.